Romance h
and she will love you forever!

LOVE

Coaching Men

YOUR

in the Art of Romance

WIFE

LANCE BROWN & CURT CAMPBELL

LOVE
YOUR
WIFE

Nashville, TN

Love Your Wife: Coaching Men in the Art of Romance

Copyright © 2021 by Lance Brown and Curt Campbell.

The Holy Bible, New International Version®, NIV® Copyright © 1973, 1978, 1984, 2011 by Biblica, Inc.® Used by permission. All rights reserved worldwide.
"New International Version" and "NIV" are registered trademarks of Biblica, Inc.®.
Used with permission.

New American Standard Bible®, Copyright © 1960, 1971, 1977, 1995 by The Lockman Foundation. All rights reserved. Used with permission.

Editorial services: Karen Carlson
Marketing services: Scott Mills
Cover, interior design, and typesetting: Lauren Murrell
Cover image: unsplash.com/@hannahbusing

ISBN: 9780977654529

First printing 2022

Printed in the United States of America

This book is dedicated to my wife and best friend. You have put up with a lot from me to get this project done and I can't thank you enough! It sounds sappy, but you really are the inspiration for this book. We always talk about never settling for an average marriage, but striving for excellence in our relationship. Thank you for working so hard to make our marriage great. You make me want to be a better man every day and in every way. I love you, Sweetness!

Lance

Pops and MuBear, for over 50 years now you have modeled a Godly marriage for me, and left an incredible legacy of love to your children and grandchildren. Thank you!

Tommy Nelson, your series on The Song of Solomon has fueled the fire in my heart to love my wife well, no matter what. Thank you for sharing your Godly wisdom and counsel. Lance and I are products of your discipleship.

Emily Anne Campbell, God blessed me beyond measure when He brought you into my life. Simply put, you just make me and my life better in every way. I love you with all of my heart! Thank you for partnering with me to make our journey the very best that it can be . . . one day at a time.

Curt

CONTENTS

Chapter 1

NOT WHAT
I EXPECTED

Lance

"How did I get here? I didn't sign up for this. Sitting in the waiting room of a counselor's office? Me? This is for husbands whose marriages are on the ropes. Guys who have been selfish, workaholics or worse . . . had affairs! But I'm in full-time ministry, I attended Promise Keepers back in the 90's and I even read my Bible every morning! How did I end up here?"

I looked over at Aimee (she was keeping her distance down at the other end of the couch from me) and she didn't look like the same woman I married. Something was missing. Not physically. She was still the beautiful girl I met in college, but her eyes just seemed dim and hollow.

It didn't start out this way. Our wedding day was amazing! I don't think my feet touched the ground. I couldn't believe I was going to get to spend the rest of my life with this girl. In college, she was the one all the guys wanted to date. She was tall, athletic, Godly and smokin' hot. Our first date was like none I had ever experienced and, you might not believe this, but I knew that was my last first date. She was the one for me . . . I just had to convince her! And the pursuit was on. I did things I used to make fun of other dudes for doing. I wrote poems. On rainy days I would wait outside the old Belmont University Humanities Building with an umbrella to walk her to her next class. I would talk to her on the phone for hours. Do I need to keep going?

The pursuit worked, and on our wedding day, as she walked down that aisle toward me, I felt like I could take on the world with this girl by my side. So that is exactly what I did. We came home from our honeymoon and I went to work and started chasing my dreams as hard and as fast I could! You add a couple of kids to the mix, fast forward a few years, and we ended up in a marriage counselor's office.

We were called back from the waiting room and somehow my mind kicked into self-protection mode. I began to reason internally that we were actually here because of Aimee, not me. As much as I didn't want to do this whole "counseling thing," I decided I should suck it up for Aimee's sake. I mean, she really had gotten off track. Sure, she felt we were there for me, something about me working too much and not listening to her . . . or at least, I think that is what she said. But I knew the truth. She needed someone, other than me, to get in her face and tell her just how good she had it. I mean when you compare me to all the other husbands this counselor dude has met with every day, I had to be a breath of fresh air for him and relieved to know there is at least one good man and great husband still out there! So, I did what any caring and serving husband would do; I followed

Aimee into the counselor's office and prayed silently that this guy would take it easy on my wife during this first session.

He asked for Aimee to share first and I thought, "This guy is good. He can tell just by looking at us who needs the most help." Imagine my shock when Aimee began to share and cry and share and cry and blame me and cry and share and blow her nose and cry. Once she had gotten it all out and polished off a box of Kleenex, it was my turn. Finally, the moment I had come here for. All along my plan had been to let this guy know what he needed to do to help Aimee and then leave them to set her next appointment so she could start her journey of recovery. But something strange happened while Aimee had been sharing and slobbering. For the first time in over two years I heard more than my wife's words. I actually heard her heart. I saw a true level of pain and hurt in her face and spirit. And like a 2x4 from the rafters of heaven, God hit me across the head and I realized no self-preserving reason could shield me from the truth . . . it was ME. I had gotten us here. I had done everything I could think of to win Aimee's heart in college, but had done very little in the last two years to keep her heart.

Time for Some Change

I left the counselor's office that day like a deer in headlights. I started the day hoping this would be Aimee's breakthrough day and our marriage could get back on track. But now the cold shower of reality was letting me know that God intended for this to be my breakthrough day.

It's not like our marriage was in horrible shape, we had made a commitment at the very beginning that the "D" word would never be an option for us (more about this later). Basically, no matter how tough it got we made a pact that we would never even say the word divorce. There have been times, however, when I'm sure Aimee has felt like

Ruth Graham did. When asked about whether she and Billy might ever divorce, Ruth Graham said, "I have never considered divorce, murder at times, but never divorce!"

So, what was I going to do? I knew a lot of men (including most of the men in my own family) who decided their marriages were too hard and too much work to expect anything more than average. And

> *"I HAVE NEVER CONSIDERED DIVORCE, MURDER AT TIMES, BUT NEVER DIVORCE!"*
> RUTH GRAHAM

great marriages were only in fairy tales and happily-ever-after movies. I really didn't want to be one of those guys who plays softball three nights a week and does the bare minimum to keep the wife and kids happy. Up to this point in my life I had strived for excellence in my education, in my work, in my church involvement and even in my friendships. Why was excellence my standard in every area of my life except my marriage? Shouldn't my marriage be done with excellence, even if it was at the expense of everything else? Not vice versa? I decided it was time to make some changes.

It Starts with the Heart

Of course, deciding to make changes and having good intentions to make some changes are great, but intentions without actions are really just good ideas that no one ever sees. The first thing that had to take place was to transfer what I knew needed to happen from my mind and have it take root in my heart. "For as he thinks within himself, so he is . . . " Proverbs 23:7 (NASB).

Too many times men are guilty of fixing their problems with a "to do" list or a set of objectives and then they go after it with the intensity of a fullback at the goal line. However, "to do" lists and goal setting are great at work, but are really cold, insincere and less than subtle at home. It makes our wives feel like just another obligation that you are trying to finish so you can check it off for the week and move on.

This is going to blow your mind, but our wives have no desire to be an obligation. No one wants things done for them out of duty or guilt. My wife wants my actions and treatment of her to come from my heart, not my daily planner. I assure you; your wife feels the same.

But I'm getting way ahead of myself. More of the whole heart vs. head discussion later. Now back to me. Remember, I have just found out, from listening to Aimee share with the counselor, that I'm the big player in why our marriage ranks as a low four on a 1 to 10

> **WHY WAS EXCELLENCE MY STANDARD IN EVERY AREA OF MY LIFE EXCEPT MY MARRIAGE?**

scale. I had been too busy to notice her needs, but I wasn't too busy to remind her of my needs. Of course, my needs are fairly simple . . . sex, sex and then after that, sex. This is where you "Amen", men!

Can You Relate?

We didn't get here overnight. Right out of college I went on staff with the Fellowship of Christian Athletes in Nashville, Tennessee. It was 1991 and I was living in my folk's basement and making $10,000 a year! That's right: 1991, not 1891, and making just $10,000. But I was in love and just wanted to save all the money I could to buy an engagement ring. So, on October 4, 1991 (the one-year anniversary of our first date) I asked Aimee Rae Smith to be my wife and she said, "Yes!"

We were married the following summer - July 11th, to be exact. Our honeymoon lasted almost two weeks and was awesome. Sanibel Island and then a few days at Disney World . . . it was magical (see what I did there). We had our whole future ahead of us and things were going perfectly. Perfectly, that is, until we came back home and reengaged in life. We had somehow thought everyday life would be like the honeymoon. You know . . . sleep late, hit the beach, back to the room for a little "play time" and cap it off with a romantic dinner for two. Am I the only guy who's ever thought that the honeymoon was how married life was going to be? Boy, was I surprised when we got back to Nashville and I had to go to work. And then to find out that sex had gone from twice a day on the honeymoon to twice a month! What the heck is this all about? Is this the "for better or worse" I heard the preacher talk about a few months ago?

Meanwhile, in Aimee's world she was wondering what the heck happened to her "beach boy", who was attentive to her every need, and took her out for romantic dinners filled with great conversation every night. Now her beach prince was leaving early, coming home late, bringing work home, announcing that eating out is too expensive and asking for clean underwear. She was shocked at how much he watched football on TV. She remembered how he liked to listen to her and actually used to ask about her day. When they dated, he would talk with her on the phone for hours. Now it was, "I'm coming home. What's for dinner? Do you need me to pick up anything?"

The honeymoon was over. Don't get me wrong, it certainly wasn't all bad. I still would try to find times to take her out for dinner or do something special within our very limited budget, but those times were stretched out over a year or more. I just wasn't as focused on Aimee as I had been when we were dating. Like most men, I thought once we got married, she would understand we were a team attacking the world together - that we were starting a new chapter as a couple. This was certainly true, but I didn't realize that each chapter of life builds on the one before. And, whatever I did in the "dating" chapter that *won* Aimee's heart was what she needed me to be doing to *keep* her heart in this new chapter!

Why Read On?

So, if you are a man whose wife would say that you are ultra-romantic and are meeting all her needs, or if she says you should write a book on romance and you are "the man" for her, then put this book down and keep on keeping on!

However, I have not met many guys like that. Most are more like me...a man who was romantic while dating and even early in the marriage, but with kids, a mortgage, work and just life in general, romance seems too hard and not really worth it. If you would rather bungee jump with too much rope off a short bridge than visit with your bride over a candlelight dinner, then it is time to read on. If you are tired of being an average man in a sub-average marriage, let's get to work!

No man I know of wakes up in the morning and says to himself, "I hope I'm mediocre today. I hope the boss finds my performance average." No, we strive for excellence. Isn't it time we start striving for excellence in the most significant arena of our life ... our home and our marriage? Why are we so content to do the minimum in this area of our lives when it deserves the maximum?

Curt and I don't have all the answers. The truth is we are both still learning and growing in our marriages. We are striving to avoid the enemies of complacency and contentment. Neither of us want a "ho-hum" average marriage, so we are constantly pursuing growth and are committed to being lifetime learners.

As Curt's friend for 20+ years (mainly because I feel sorry for the dude), I assure you he will make feeble attempts at humor, but he will also have some great insights

> *WHY ARE WE SO CONTENT TO DO THE MINIMUM IN THIS AREA OF OUR LIVES WHEN IT DESERVES THE MAXIMUM?*

that will challenge us in regard to loving our wives in a more intentional and romantic way.

Join us as we trash talk, bash each other, brag about our successes, cry over our failures, and learn together. Our hope is that you will, at a minimum, finish this book with a renewed commitment to romance your bride, to sweep her off her feet and make her glad she said, "I do!"

✓ Action Step

Don't be afraid of getting help. Don't let your ego be the reason you lose your marriage. An older Christian couple or a Christian marriage counselor can offer some great insight into how you can maximize your marriage. You may simply need a tune up or an oil change, or you may need a complete overhaul. Wherever you are in your relationship with your wife, just make sure you are doing regular maintenance on your marriage.

▶ Romance Tip

List of Positive Attributes
https://www.youtube.com/watch?v=yuPC4sTjxLg

Chapter 2

IS *THIS* MY
LIFE...REALLY?

Curt

Not bad, LB... thank God for people with the gift of editing! This co-write may work after all. Just kidding, man – I'm grateful for your willingness to be honest and candid about your journey in marriage. One of the greatest encouragements to me throughout our friendship has been the complete transparency at the gut level. The good, the bad, the ugly – let's call it what it is and keep working to get better as husbands!

When Lance was telling me about being in the counseling office with Aimee, it brought back some memories of the early years with Emily. Two things came immediately to mind – one was a journal entry I made not too far into marriage, and the other was a phone conversation I had with my parents while sitting in the Lowe's Home

Improvement parking lot in Madison, Tennessee. I remember it like it was yesterday. Here's a portion of the journal entry:

> March 28, 2003
> I can't believe I'm writing this, but I really think this is going to be my life. I don't know how to connect with Emily. She is not the easy-going, laid back woman I married. She is snappy, shut-down, cold and disengaged. She is aware of it, but she's either unable or unwilling to change. She keeps saying she's going to snap out of it, but she's been saying that for well over a year now. I can't convince her to go to counseling. I think this is my lot in life. God, I'm going to need your help. Most days I feel like I'm walking on egg shells - I never know who I am coming home to anymore. I am sad for her, for us. I'm angry, but I'm not sure who to be mad at. God, I'm in this for better or for worse, and I'm not going anywhere, but I never dreamed it could be like this. Give me strength for the journey.

Just a little over a year into our marriage, things started to go south . . . and I don't mean Georgia – more like just north of Hell (at least it felt that way). One of my names for Emily has always been "Sweet Em". She was easygoing, peaceful, and truly sweet to the core. Everybody has their bad days, of course, but these endearing qualities were definitely the pattern of her life – a huge part of the reason I married her. In addition, of course, to her Godly character and looks that have made many (and, I do mean many) heads turn to the point of wrenching vertebrae. I'm distracted now – forgive me.

Anyway, a *new* pattern developed. It developed quickly, without warning, and it was not subtle, and was anything but "sweet". Suddenly, she was chronically tired, very irritable, snappy, and pessimistic. She was not happy with her life, herself, and it certainly seemed she was not happy with me. This affected everything – the climate of our home, the way we communicated (or didn't), and certainly brought our affection and sex life to a screeching halt. She could not put into words what was wrong, regardless of how much I pursued. I suggested counseling, to no avail. She saw a couple of doctors to see if there might be a medical issue, but bloodwork came back normal. This was uncharted territory for both of us – a dark place, getting darker, with no apparent light at the end of the tunnel. When we did talk about it, her standard and hopeful response was, "I'll snap out of it."

Only a couple of years into marriage, and just a little over a year into this daily routine of misery, I called my folks from the Lowe's Home Improvement parking lot in Madison, Tennessee, with a broken heart and an admission that I was going to have to just accept this was my lot in life. I was committed to loving Emily well, regardless of how she treated me. I didn't understand it, but I did believe God would strengthen me for the journey one day at a time. I had a sense of resolve, but my heart was broken. It was broken for me. It was broken for Emily. And it was broken for our kids, who were also bearing the brunt of "Mom's" unhappiness, fatigue and irritability.

I had recently memorized I Corinthians 10:13, which says, "No temptation has seized you except what is common to man. And God is faithful: He will not let you be tempted beyond what you can bear. But when you are tempted, He will also provide a way out so that you can stand up under it." I believed this, since it was in God's Word, but the temptation to shut down and just do me was very real and very strong. I had to rely on the Truth of God's Word, I had to apply it, and I desperately needed to be around people who were encouraging me to stay the course and love Emily through this very difficult time.

Like Lance and Aimee, divorce was never an option for us. We made that decision before we ever got married. But shutting down, isolating, and becoming self-focused was unfortunately a daily choice, and one I am ashamed to say I made on way too many occasions. These choices, no doubt, prolonged and perpetuated the downward spiral of our marriage.

A Sense of Resolve

As you've read these last few paragraphs, you've probably been focused on me and how I was feeling through all of this. Guess what . . . I was, too. Let's push the pause button on the "woe is me" "pity party for Curt" portion of this chapter and consider for a moment what my wife was experiencing. Can you imagine living with these thoughts day in and day out?

"I don't have the energy to do anything."
"I may never feel good again."
"I am a terrible wife and mother."
"I am ugly inside and out."
"My husband regrets marrying me."
"My children wish they had a different mom."
"Everyone would be happier if I wasn't here."

Will you please go back and read those thoughts again and imagine living in that mindset for any period of time? My coldness, isolation, and repeated failed attempts to have *my needs* met just slid us further and further down the hole. I was completely ignorant to the fact that I was re-enforcing all of Emily's negative thoughts by my actions. Instead, I should have been working hard to convince her I loved her unconditionally and assuring her we would get through this. That whole "for better or for worse, in sickness and in health, 'til death do us part" thing was just something we said at the altar, wasn't it? I never imagined what it meant to actually live out our vows.

Without belaboring the point, let me just share with you that about two years after Emily started tanking, we finally discovered she had a hyper-thyroid. Imagine that...it wasn't that she wanted to be miserable and wanted everyone else to be miserable with her; she had a hormonal imbalance that caused her body to be working over-time, ALL of the time. She was legitimately exhausted, continually, for two years. It almost makes me cry, even now, to write this. Man, I missed an opportunity to serve her and minister to her when she needed me most! It breaks my heart! I'm going to stop writing and apologize, again...be right back.

(Okay. She forgave me, again. Thank you, Emily. You are so gracious toward me.)

She had her thyroid removed, and as the doctors worked over the next several weeks to get her on the right number of daily hormones, she once again became my "Sweet Em". Let me assure you, though, I learned a very significant lesson in all of this that served me well a few years later – I'll tell you about that in a future chapter. But here's the lesson: "Fulfilling my role and responsibility in marriage as a husband is not dependent on my wife fulfilling her role." I have learned I really can find great satisfaction in marriage just by being the husband I committed to being.

Let's try that one more time . . . not just for you, but for Lance. And for me, too, of course.

> *Fulfilling my role and my responsibility in marriage as a husband is not dependent on my wife fulfilling her role.*

Does that sound like resolve? It sounds like resolve to me. I don't give love to my wife based on what I'm receiving from her. I love her, period. Without expectation. Is this difficult to do? You know, it is and it isn't. Our needs as men are real, and we'll talk in a later chapter about how to effectively communicate those needs and prayerfully get them met.

But what I've found in this resolution to love my wife, no matter what, is an amazing sense of freedom and purpose. It has somewhat become my identity. And Emily knows it. It reminds me of a song lyric talking about loving and serving your wife. It says,

> *"It won't ever get much easier. We're all selfish through and through. But if you'll spend a lifetime lovin' her, I bet she'll do the same for you."*

Talk about a marriage made in Heaven . . . me doing everything I can to love and serve Emily and Emily doing everything she can to love and serve me. What if I told you that actually is the concept of marriage that *was made* in Heaven?

Keep reading . . . it gets better! If Lance has quit daydreaming, and you can weed through Chapter 3, I'll be back in Chapter 4 to bring some clarity.

✓ Action Step

Love your wife out of a grateful heart for the way God loves you. Look for ways to serve, honor, and respect her without expecting anything in return.

For some helpful ideas, check out the Game Plans on our website: *www.loveyourwife.net.*

▶ Romance Tip

 **"Note on Mirror"**

https://www.youtube.com/watch?v=wVwSSPTcqkw

Chapter 3

MUSTS FOR MEN
IN MARRIAGE

Lance

Curt, the reason I am daydreaming is because your writing puts me in a semi-conscious state! Good stuff in that chapter, though, and glad that God AND Emily got a hold of you and set you straight. Now let's see if we can help you men with some X's and O's for marriage . . .

My church had one of those men's conferences. You know, one of those deals where the church starts promoting it several weeks out, but no one signs up. Well, actually there are the few guys who are on the sign-up list, but those are the guys whose wives filled out the forms and paid the conference fee. Imagine their surprise when they get their confirmation email and the conference schedule! So, with just a handful of men registered and the conference only a week away, our pastor gets up and questions the manhood of all the men in the congregation and whether they love their wives, children and country. This passionate plea still doesn't get men to give up a Friday night and all-day Saturday to have someone tell them how sorry they are.

What it takes is some drastic measures by the wives. They threaten to either cutoff sex (which for some men it might take a few weeks to notice this tactic), or they cancel the cable sports package for the upcoming NFL season. The ladies sure do know how to motivate us men, because when I showed up for the opening session on Friday night the church parking lot was packed and over 1,000 men were in attendance! You see, when men are faced with no sex and no sports, they are willing to sign away their first-born child to appease their wives!

For this particular men's conference my church asked me to lead a breakout session on how to treat your wife. I am going to share a few things in this chapter I shared that night, but I have to make a confession, many of the points have been gleaned from years of using Tommy Nelson's series on Song of Solomon as a required curriculum for every couple I have led through pre-marriage counseling. So, with appropriate credit going to Tommy here we go . . .

Flowers and chocolates are enough . . . right?!

Romance DOES NOT stop at the altar; it is actually only beginning! Whatever we did to win our wife's heart during the dating and courtship stages are the very things we must continue to do to keep our wife's heart (this quote may be getting old, but most of us have to see and hear something over and over for it to take).

For many men the dating scene is like a hunt. They go out into the natural habitat of the woman, or at least where they hope to find several gathered (now they troll date apps). They ease up to one who seems friendly . . . all the while hoping they don't spook her and make her run away. And then they use their limited relationship skills like romance, conversation and charm to win her over. However, once once they've won her heart and get married, the most romantic thing they do is let her watch "The Bachelor" on the big screen in the man cave once a week while he works late at the office!

It is interesting that the most common excuse I hear for why men don't continue to romance their wives is, "I'm not a very romantic guy." Funny, you were a regular Don Juan when you were dating her. You were writing poetry like a Hallmark card author and buying flowers for no reason. Plus, have you ever stopped to consider that much of the top poetry and art in our world has been done by men? Many of them were even married men! What does that tell us? Men have been given the God-ordained ability to be creative and romantic!

Why do we not continue to romance our wives?

- Because we begin to take them for granted.
- They become convenient and we assume they will always be there.
- We think that providing financial security is all we need to do to keep them happy. What more could they possibly want than a house, a car and some clothes?
- We just don't have the time, or the energy, required for romancing our wives any more.

Almost all men will agree we find time for the things most important to us. We find time for golf. We find time for ESPN. We find time for Netflix. We find time for our kids. Many of us even find time for church. Yet our brides have to settle for the crumbs and leftovers from the table of our busy agendas. Does this seem like the way God intended marriage to be? I hope you agree it is not.

This leaves us with one conclusion. We don't romance our wives anymore because she just isn't as important as she used to be. "Wait a minute Lance, you can't say that to me! I love my wife." I didn't say you didn't love her. I said she is no longer important to you. "Yes, she is, I love her."

OUR BRIDES HAVE TO SETTLE FOR THE CRUMBS AND LEFTOVERS FROM THE TABLE OF OUR BUSY AGENDAS.

Well, if she is important to you, and you love her, then does she know that? Better yet, do you really think she FEELS she is important to you? When was the last time you put her before your work, or before the kids, or before YOU?

You better plant some roses; you are going to need them!

Winning Is Overrated!

Another area where we tend to fail is how we speak to our brides when we are "discussing" something. Okay, let's not call it discussing, let's call it disagreeing, arguing or UFC cage fighting! In other words, how do you speak to your wife when you are in the middle of an argument? That is when we find out who's a boy, who's a man, but really who is a *gentle*-man.

In most cases, men are able to compartmentalize our emotions. What I mean is we can take how we feel and put it in boxes. We take bad news and swallow it, put it in the bad news box, go to the big presentation meeting and act like it is the best day of our lives and then deal with the bad news later. I have heard our wives' emotions described more like a river. They all flow together. For this reason, it is important for us to be the anchor in the middle of that river. Not a stubborn immovable object, but a safe and secure anchor to grasp during the stresses of parenting and marriage. Our wives need us to hold things in place in the midst of the raging rapids of life.

However, many of us have chosen to join the storm and rage against our wives in the hopes they will cave and then we win . . . but what exactly have we won? Let's be honest, we know if we yell a little louder or come off a little more forceful, she will probably back down. There are a lot of guys out there who have been using this tactic with their wives for years. Some have even resorted to physical assault to win. If this is you, let me be clear . . . you are NOT a man! You are a boy. Get away from your wife and kids until you can get some real help with your temper.

Others may not get physical, but it is not any better when we raise our voices or demean our wives to get the victory. Let me ask you to look over your shoulder as you are walking out of the room feeling like you won something. Tell me what you see. Sure, you just made your point, but at what cost? You took the most precious gift God has ever given you and just crushed it so you could get a win. Help me understand how that is a victory? How that makes you a man?

Adapted from a Tommy Nelson (Senior Pastor, Denton Bible Church) list, here are some important things to keep in mind when you and your wife are communicating:

DO	DON'T
Be kind with your words	Be harsh/rude
Handle conflict in private	Embarrass her publicly
Keep children out of marital conflict	Create fear, anxiety and insecurity, which can force a child to choose sides
Use words like "rarely"/"sometimes"	Use words like "never"/"always"
Choose to forgive and forget	Bring up past wrongs
Keep your composure	Raise your voice
Attack the problem	Attack the person
Seek to reconcile	Seek to win

With all that in mind, when we are in an argument with our brides, we (men) need to be the leaders. We need to be the calming force in the storm. We need to respond and not react. Reacting is when your wife raises her voice and says something about your momma and then you react back by yelling at the top of your lungs and questioning why she was even born. Ok, that might be extreme, but you get my point. Responding is maintaining your composure as your wife express-es her frustration with whatever emotion she may have in the moment and then responding with as much grace as you can draw from God. How in the world do you maintain your com-posure in the midst of chaos? The best soldiers do it on the battlefield and the top athletes do it in the arena of com-petition. It is keeping your head while everyone else is losing theirs (I wouldn't read this sentence to your wife)!

WHAT IF WINNING IS NOT YOU WINNING, BUT WE WINNING?

I really want to challenge you to redefine winning when it comes to arguing with your wife. What if winning is not *you* winning, but *we* winning? I know, I know, compromise is for the weak and the loser. But remember, this isn't PlayStation and Xbox. This is your wife, your bride, your special gift from God almighty. Is being right more important than her heart?

Sex has nothing to do with you

Ok men, let's take a quick look at our favorite subject…sex! For women sex is very emotional. They need to feel connected on non-physical levels before they surrender themselves sexually. Huh? What in the world are non-physical levels? Is that like kissing her without grabbing at her? No, it is more like actually communicating with her like a real person! Yes, I said it. You need to talk with your wife. Ask her about her day, and then listen to her response! Good grief, Lance, what does this have to do with sex? Everything. Foreplay starts sometimes days before the actual event.

I don't want to brag, but I have some foreplay techniques that have produced some amazing results! I have asked Aimee's permission to share some of those maneuvers with you in this book, but I do ask that you respect our privacy and not share them with anyone else. Ok, are you sure you're ready? One time I took out the trash, did the dishes after dinner and then put the kids to bed for Aimee. Another time I folded the laundry. Oh yeah, and then there was the day I sat and rubbed her feet and just talked with her about her day and the kid's activities. I'm telling you . . . she went wild!

Why does all that sound stupid to us? Because for men to be in the mood for sex, all we need is to be naked and even that is not really necessary! I believe Gary Smalley was the first to say that women heat up like crock pots, it may take all day, but it sure is worth it. But men are like microwaves, "Ding!" and we are overheated and fully cooked. Unfortunately, we are done about as fast as a microwave as well!

We must get over ourselves and this male ego thing that says we are some kind of amazing lover who our wives should be begging to be with every night. Sex is not about you. Sex is about your bride. It is arguably one of the greatest gifts God gives a husband and wife to enjoy, but it is intended for those who are unselfish and are looking to the needs and desires of their mate. It is not about you getting your needs met, it is all about you pleasing and meeting the needs of your bride. And sometimes that starts with taking out the trash!

You Better Meet Her Needs or Someone Else Will!

Early in our marriage, Aimee and I read the book "His Needs, Her Needs" by Willard Harley. In the book, Harley shares from his years of marriage counseling about five basic needs of men and five basic needs of women. The irony is that the respective needs of a man and a woman could not be much different from each other. This book was so good for us in the early years of marriage. We really jumped in and worked hard to meet each other's needs. And it truly gave us a good foundation as a new married couple.

However, looking back I'm not sure if my motives were always the purest in trying to meet Aimee's needs. You see, growing up in a home where my father had an affair while I was still in my mother's womb, there were some subconscious fears of not meeting one of Aimee's needs and her going elsewhere to have those needs met. As I look back on our marriage, those fears were foolish. My wife is the most loyal woman of God and would never do something like that. My other, less than appealing, motive for meeting Aimee's needs was the hope that if I met Aimee's needs, she would feel obligated to meet my needs.

Although Harley's book is very true in saying we each have needs we would like to have met, marriage is far more than "you scratch my back and I will scratch yours." Knowing the five basic needs of Aimee gave me a list to work from, but it still had to come from my heart. It still came down to meeting those needs from a pure motive.

Do you know when I feel like I'm closest to having the right motive and heart about meeting Aimee's needs? It's when I meet her needs and I'm not mad, frustrated, angry or disappointed if my needs are not met in return. Or even better, when I meet her needs and my efforts go unnoticed or unappreciated . . . and I'm okay with it. Then I know my heart and motives are about my bride and her happiness.

Yes, we need to be looking to satisfy the extrinsic and intrinsic desires of our wives. But it only counts if we are meeting those needs for the purpose of bringing a smile to her face and joy to her world.

Once again, fellas, this is not about us. It is not about us getting what we want. We are called to love her like Christ loved us . . . which brings up words like: servant, sacrifice, care, unconditional, forgiving and gracious. Not exactly the kinds of things you are taught in business school. But then again, this isn't about financial statements and bottom lines; this is about loving and cherishing God's gift.

Looks Don't Last

If it was all about looks, who should have the best marriages? Hollywood. But who has the worst marriages? Hollywood. Why? Curt and I have heard Tommy Nelson say many times, "Bad character always voids good looks."

Have you ever seen that couple who just doesn't match up? How does this happen? It looks like one of those online match maker sites had a virus! Sure, it could also be that this gorgeous woman is with this short, balding, slightly overweight guy because he is swimming in money. However, in most cases it is because women have once again learned something us men have yet to figure out. Looks fade, but character stays.

Don't get me wrong. My wife is one hot babe. Aimee is actually the exception to the point I'm trying to make. The two of us are like wine and cheese. She is getting better and better with age and all I am doing is getting moldy and smelly! I'm fully prepared for the day when Aimee and I go out for dinner and the waitress turns to me and says, "You must be so proud to have such a beautiful daughter".

Every morning, I'm reminded that looks don't last when I get out of the shower and leave behind what has become one of my most prized possessions . . . my hair! Or when I turn and look in the mirror and my former six pack has become a keg with a belly button that could easily be mistaken as the hole for the spout.

Here's the deal men: don't let yourself go. I'm not talking about physically here, although most of us could stand to lose a few; I'm talking about our character. Our wives certainly want us to stay in shape and look good. But they can cope with physical atrophy a whole lot easier than a man who lacks integrity or just basic kindness. Our wives need men who are noble. Men who look to do the right thing. Men who they can point their children to and say, "Just watch your daddy and live how he lives and you will be fine".

Chick Flicks Aren't Enough

Aimee loves to go to movies. She is a huge Tyler Perry and "Madea" fan. I have to admit it's funny to see this suburban, white middle-class church going woman bust out in her Madea impersonations. What makes it even funnier is that she is pretty good at it.

Can I admit something that I hope Curt doesn't read? Aimee and I will watch the movie "The Notebook" at least three times a year. I'm a hopeless romantic and that is the best chick flick of all time! By the way, "Pride and Prejudice" is a close second.

As much as I like to watch "The Notebook" and other movies with Aimee, it is not enough. She needs me to spend time with her every day. She wants to do something called conversation. I know you may not have heard of this, or you may think conversation consists of the weather and the top 10 plays from SportsCenter this morning. However, this huge word, *conversation*, is what women do a lot of with each other when we men aren't around. It is something they really enjoy doing and they are very proficient in this art.

Unfortunately, this is not something you can do while watching TV or surfing social media. It is an acquired skill. It requires us to listen and then give more than a one syllable answer. It is a very demanding artform and can really push men to our limits!

I can guess what you are thinking at this point . . . "Okay, Lance, I'm out! I was open to the whole romance thing and meeting needs and sex, but now you have crossed the line. You actually want me to carry on an adult conversation with my wife, where I listen, act interested and give profound feedback so I can 'deepen our relationship'? Where did I put the receipt for this book? It might not be too late to return it."

Find a brown bag and take a few deep breaths in it! Relax and keep reading. Now, I need to ask you something I have already asked earlier, but needs repeating. Are you content to be average at work? I mean, do you get up in the mornings, shower, shave and get dressed, then head out the door in pursuit of mediocrity? You would not be reading this book if that's who you are. No, real men want to be the best. We are by nature competitive and we want to be the best at work and at play. If your boss needed you to take a customer to dinner and connect with them before the big presentation, you would not reply with "I am not really good at connecting or talking". No, you would find a way. Why? Because you want to be great at what you do. Guess what . . . the greatest place you can be great as a man is being an intentional and pursuant husband to your wife! You can just talk TO your wife about the house, kids and work . . . average. Or you can talk WITH your wife about her dreams, goals and life . . . excellence. You choose.

In case you choose excellence, here are some more pointers from (you guessed it) Tommy Nelson:

- Put your phone and remote away. Have a little bucket or basket to put ALL phones in and be intentional about old school facetime!
- We may be in problem solving mode all day at work, but don't bring that mindset home! Most of the time she knows

how to fix her problems, she just wants you to listen, not try to fix everything.

- Keep your composure and tone so you can discuss, not argue. No one is listening when everyone is arguing.
- Let her finish what she is saying. It is frustrating to anyone to be interrupted. (This is my toughest one. I interrupt Aimee often and regret it every time.)
- Stay in the discussion. Leaving before a talk is over or because you're not winning is what two-year-olds do. Staying to the end says, "I will not walk out on you. I am here until we find a solution. I won't go to bed angry."
- My grandfather used to say, "Don't put your business on the street." I think what he meant was to not go vent all your stuff to anyone who will listen. You and your wife will hopefully work through an issue and kiss and make-up, but if you have bashed her to a bunch of your friends they will grow to dislike her and hold things against her because they weren't part of your resolution, only the venting.
- Did you know that most experts agree that 70-93% of communication is non-verbal? What does your body language say to your wife? Folded arms say, "I am shutting down and closed to what you are saying." Rolling the eyes says, "What you just said is stupid or dramatic and I will not validate your feelings because they are absurd." Sighing or huffing (I do this one) says, "I really don't have time for this and you are really irritating me right now."

NO ONE IS LISTENING WHEN EVERYONE IS ARGUING.

Not Yet Curt!

Before you are bored to sleep by Curt in the next chapter, please take a moment to think about an area in the "Musts for Men" that you need to work on. Now go do it! But make sure you are doing it from your heart and not from your "to-do" list. You want your wife to feel loved and cherished, not like a deadline on your calendar! See you men again in Chapter 5!

✔️ Action Point

Go back and look at the list on communication and the list on listening. Choose one point from each list, and this week make a conscience and intentional effort to communicate differently and listen better! What if you asked your wife to share her biggest fear or a dream she thinks will never happen? Then, with phone and remote in a bucket, just look her in the face and listen. Listen beyond what she is saying and hear her heart.

▶️ Romance Tip

"Sticky Notes"

https://www.youtube.com/watch?v=4KWWVxm-svQ

Chapter 4

IT'S ALL ABOUT
ME, RIGHT?

Curt ———————————————————————————————

Is anyone else asking themselves why I didn't just ask Tommy Nelson to co-write this book with me? Sorry, Tommy . . . had I known where we were headed with this, I could have cut out the middle man. But seriously, Lance and I both have been students under Tommy's tutelage for years. We would both highly recommend his series called, "The Song of Solomon, A Study of Love, Sex, Romance and Marriage."

Can we start this chapter with a pretty shocking and revealing statistic? Did you know there are over 26 million arranged marriages every year? Do you have any idea what percentage of those marriages end in divorce? Are you ready for this? Only 4% of arranged marriages worldwide end in divorce. For you guys who flunked Math, that's a 96% success rate when someone other than you chooses your spouse and you enter into a marriage covenant. That seems crazy, doesn't it?

When you consider the typically lengthy process of dating and courtship in the United States before someone actually chooses a spouse, isn't it a little surprising our divorce rate in the good ol' US of A stands close to 50% annually?

Hmmm . . . 96 out of 100 arranged marriages last. 50 out of 100 marriages based on personal choice last. That certainly begs the question, "Why?" I'd love for you to think about it for a minute before I share some insight. Why do you think this statistic remains consistent year after year around the world?

I'd like to offer it is perhaps largely due to the perspective of the people who are getting married. Most people in the United States approach dating with a very self-centered agenda. "I want to meet someone who:

1. I'm really attracted to
2. Makes me feel good
3. Mostly thinks like I do
4. Is supportive of me
5. Has similar interests as me
6. Is committed to me
7. I can grow old with

Would you agree? Do those seven things resonate with you when you think about why you married your spouse? Be honest. I would certainly say that Emily checked all seven of those boxes for me before I asked her to marry me. All right, let's do a quick breakdown on the pronouns in those seven requirements:

1. I
2. Me
3. I
4. Me
5. Me
6. Me
7. I

"Yeah, so what," you say. "What's wrong with that?" Well, here's the problem . . . if my love for my spouse, and my commitment to marriage, is based on her ability to continually check these boxes for me, I am in deep, deep trouble. If you've been married for any length of time at all, you know there are going to be plenty of days when the first five requirements listed above are going to be "iffy" at best.

1. Someone I'm really attracted to
2. Makes me feel good
3. Mostly thinks like I do
4. Is supportive of me
5. Has similar interests as me

That makes requirements 6 and 7 . . .

6. Is committed to me
7. I can grow old with

. . . questionable suddenly, and we begin to wonder if perhaps we made a mistake and chose the wrong partner. Once doubt creeps in, we can easily start to panic, get angry, shut down, look to have those "requirements" met elsewhere, and then, look out! Here we go . . . if divorce is an option, it's pretty much inevitable. I know there's more to it than that, but hopefully you get the picture. If my concept of a successful and fulfilling marriage is me getting my needs met by my spouse, I'm probably not going to have a successful or fulfilling marriage. At least not for any sustainable length of time.

Let's Say It *Is* About Me

All right, let's twist this a little bit and see if we can't challenge each other and have a little fun. If we want to make marriage about us, then let's think about it through a different lens for a minute. Now, I'm confident not every guy reading this book has read the Bible. Some of you may not know much, if anything, about a man named Jesus. He claimed to be the Son of God, and if you do the research, there is an astounding amount of evidence to suggest that He is, indeed, the Son of God. I confess that through studying about Him, as well as living through a myriad of personal experiences, I have come to a strong personal conviction He is, indeed, who He says He is. Now, if you differ in your belief, please don't quit on me here. This argument for marriage is strong whether you believe in Jesus or not. I just wanted to give you some context for the position.

> *IF MY CONCEPT OF A SUCCESSFUL AND FULFILLING MARRIAGE IS ME GETTING MY NEEDS MET BY MY SPOUSE, I'M PROBABLY NOT GOING TO HAVE A SUCCESSFUL OR FULFILLING MARRIAGE.*

So, in the Bible, in the book of Romans, the 8th chapter, the author, Paul, suggests that one of the main purposes of our having a relationship with Jesus is for us to become like Him. He is in the process of conforming us to His image. His image? What does that mean, exactly? Well, very simply, someone's image is what they look like, right? Yes, but I'm not talking about having long hair, dark skin, leather sandals, a robe and Jewish features. So, what *does* it mean for me to look like Jesus? I'm talking about lifestyle and character. And for the purposes of this book, specifically, what would it mean for me to look like Jesus in my marriage? Guys, this is about to get good. It's more than good. It is life changing!

I want you to read this verse very deliberately:

> *Romans 5:8 (NASB) "But God demonstrates His own love toward*
> *us in that while we were still sinners, Christ died for us."*

Did you catch that? We were sinning. Not just sinning in general, but specifically against God. I was (and honestly still am on a regular basis) deliberately doing things against God's will. Hurting Him. Ignoring Him. Doing what I want to do instead of what He wants me to do. In the midst of that, Jesus has done something truly unbelievable. He died for me. Literally laid down His life to put me back into good graces with God. Here's what's going to blow your mind . . . did you know on several occasions in the Bible, Jesus is referred to as our groom? If I am a Believer in Jesus, He is considered my husband. I am referred to as the bride of Christ. We're going to explore this in greater detail in a later chapter, but here's a simple summary:

1. I am to conform (with His help) to the image of Jesus in my marriage.
2. In my relationship with Him, He is the groom, I am the bride.
3. As His bride, I have hurt, ignored, and disrespected Him.
4. As my Groom, He has forgiven me repeatedly and completely. He gave His life for mine.

Remember, read this deliberately with "conforming to the image of Jesus" in mind as a husband.

> *"In your relationships with one another, have the same mindset as Christ Jesus: Who, being in very nature, God, did not consider equality with God something to be used to his own advantage; rather he made himself nothing by taking the very nature of a servant, being made in human likeness. And being found in appearance as a man, he humbled himself by becoming obedient to death — even death on a cross."*
> *Philippians 2:5-8 (NIV)*

Service and Humility

Now, whether you believe it, or not, let's just say for the sake of argument that Jesus is the Son of God. If anyone deserves to be treated like a King, it would be Him. He should be pampered, honored, respected, served, and the list would go on and on. Don't you agree? That we, as His bride, should put Him first in every single instance? His way or the highway! But I certainly don't do that. And, I'd place a pretty hefty bet you don't either. With that being the case, wouldn't you think He would smite us and just wipe us off the face of the earth? If He is God, He certainly could. Or perhaps, in context, it would definitely be within His rights to reject us or divorce us with his arms crossed in contempt, wouldn't it?

IF YOU WANT TO MAKE MARRIAGE ABOUT YOU, MAKE IT ABOUT YOU BEING CONFORMED TO THE IMAGE OF JESUS.

Look at His response . . . . He doesn't treat us the way we treat Him. It's not why He came as our Groom. He came to serve in humility. He came to woo us to Himself over and over again. And He does so regardless of how we treat Him.

Gentlemen, this is what being a husband looks like. Isn't it beautiful? If you want to make marriage about you, make it about *you* being conformed to the image of Jesus. Start loving your wife like Jesus loves you . . . ALL of the time! Even when your wife hurts you, ignores you, or disrespects you – respond with the love and the servant heart of Jesus.

Unfortunately, unless you're part of a very small and select group on the planet, you don't know I moved to Nashville in 1992 to be a songwriter. Yeah, that's right . . . you don't know because I never gained much notoriety as a songwriter. But I did write several hundred songs. If you'd like to *hear* the song I wrote as you read the lyrics below, you can open this QR code to the YouTube lyric video of "Love Comes from Livin'." It was inspired by this concept of loving and serving your wife, and sung by a good buddy of mine, Paul Bogart.

Love Comes from Livin'
On one of the greatest days of my life, my grandpa said,
"Son, let me tell you two things:
one, greater love hath no man
than he lay down his life for another.
And two, sometimes layin'
down your life means puttin' her first."
The best advice I ever got

Has been the toughest fight I ever fought
I've been fighting since the day I said, "I do"
Granddaddy said, "Son, most men are glad to die
For the one they love if it comes time
But love comes from livin', for her and not for you"

Chorus 1

"So, take thirty seconds to walk around the truck
Open the door and help her up
Sure son, she can do it
But she might like a helpin' hand
And if she takes the time to cook a meal
Thank her for your dinner and eat your fill
But don't ever leave the kitchen when there's dishes left to do
'Cause love comes from livin', love comes from livin'
Yeah love comes from livin', for her and not for you"

"Someday when you're old and gray
You'll know exactly what to say
When folks ask how love can last a whole life through
Just tell 'em on the day I said, 'I do'
My granddaddy passed down some truth
He said, 'love comes from livin' for her and not for you'"

Chorus 2

So, turn the TV off on Saturday
Take the kids outside to play
Help them pick some flowers
Just to brighten up her room
Rent a chick flick and hold her hand

Get your honey do's done as quick as you can
And be content with cuddlin'
When she's not quite in the mood
'Cause love comes from livin', loves comes from livin'
Yeah love comes from livin' for her and not for you"

Tag

It won't ever get much easier
We're all selfish through and through
But if you'll spend a lifetime pleasin' her
I bet she'll do the same for you

The toughest fight I've ever fought
Was the best advice I ever got

I'm sure there are some exceptions, guys, there always are. But I have seen it over and over again . . . men who relentlessly love their wives with kindness, gentleness, service, and forgiveness have the kind of marriages we all dream of. They are content with this simple goal: "It's about me . . . *becoming like Christ.*"

> MEN WHO RELENTLESSLY LOVE THEIR WIVES WITH KINDNESS, GENTLENESS, SERVICE, AND FORGIVENESS HAVE THE KIND OF MARRIAGES WE ALL DREAM OF.

✔ Action Point

Start each day this week by praying and asking God to help you fully understand how He loves you. As you receive His patience, His forgiveness, His pursuing of you, His presence, and His unconditional love, look for ways to offer those same things to your wife. Both of you will be blessed . . . I assure you!

▶ Romance Tip

"Bubble Bath"

https://www.youtube.com/watch?v=EIj5jlGXeHE

Chapter 5

ROSES AREN'T
ENOUGH

Lance ──────────────────────────

*Curt, I have to give it to you on that chapter. It is true the more I work on ME
the happier SHE will be! The blame game has been going on since the garden of
Eden. Owning our part is hard to do, but this is what separates the men from the
boys. Now let's go back to the chalkboard (dry erase board just doesn't sound right
to me) and look at some more X's and O's...*

"How high maintenance can one woman be? I mean what more
does she want from me?"

You men know this scene, don't you? You take the time to go by
Kroger on your way home, you pick up some flowers and then toss them
on the counter as you enter the back door on your way to the fridge to
get an ice-cold Diet Mtn. Dew (my beverage of choice these days).

Your expectation, as you turn around from the fridge, is to hear
soft Hallmark movie music in the background as she hugs and kisses

you and begins to gush about how awesome, romantic and thoughtful you are as a man. However, something goes terribly wrong. She doesn't seem appreciative at all. She actually appears to be irritated . . . even put out with you. How can this be?

Sometimes our intentions may be noble, but our delivery is the issue. Don't be as dumb as a friend of mine who did all the things mentioned above and then came in the house and handed his wife the flowers and said, "There, that should satisfy you for a few weeks. I did my job as a husband. Consider yourself romanced, babe!" Seriously, his intentions may have been noble, but his delivery was fatal . . . literally!

Why do we think all it takes is flowers? Or chocolate? Or diamonds (although my wife says diamonds would cover a multitude of sins)? We (men) have been dumping flowers and gifts on our wives for years in hopes of getting either forgiveness or permission. Forgiveness for going to play golf last Saturday or permission to go fishing this coming Saturday! Pop quiz time, men. If you were to bring flowers home to your wife today, which of the following reactions would best describe her?

"What did you do wrong this time?"
This wife only gets flowers for apologizes or to prepare her for a future violation – *"I Am Sorry" flowers*.

"Wait, what is today?"
This wife only gets flowers on birthdays, Valentine's Day, and maybe Mother's Day – *"Special Event" flowers*.

"Not tonight!"
This wife only gets flowers when her husband wants sex – *"Let's Get Ready to Rumble" flowers*.

"You are so sweet!"

This wife gets flowers at random times just because he loves her and intentionally expresses his love when she least expects it — *"Because I Love You" flowers.*

So, how did you do on the pop quiz? Don't worry men, none of us get this right all the time. The real point of all this is not about flowers and gifts, but more about your wife feeling loved without the flowers and gifts. Don't get me wrong, there is never a bad time to give our wives a gift! However, how can we make them feel special without the roses and diamonds? Honestly, the answer is in some old school principles that we have gotten away from as a society. It is time to call men back to chivalry and being a gentleman.

The Lost Art of Chivalry

When did it become uncool to treat ladies like ladies? With each passing decade the number of fatherless homes continues to grow. And even in the homes where there is a dad present, there's still the issue of workaholics and fathers who think financial provision is all that is required of him in regards to his wife and kids.

In my world of college athletics, I developed three core values I have spent the last 15+ years teaching young college male athletes. Core Values:

1. Be Gentlemen
2. Be Men of Integrity
3. Display Moral Courage

If you are interested in knowing more about these values, then stay tuned; that is my next book project (I hope). But here I want to talk about being a gentleman. The very word defines itself . . . gentle-man.

But how do you define or even explain the word gentleman when they have not seen this modeled for them at home? What I do know is that although many of today's young men have grown up in homes with no father, they have had a strong, sacrificial single-mom who has stepped in the gap and filled both roles in raising these boys to become men. And for this reason, these young men have grown to be very protective of their mommas, and rightfully so! With this knowledge, I decided to define being a gentleman as "treating a young lady the way you would want a man to treat your own momma". This seems to get their attention, but we still have work to do.

There has to be a way to illustrate to men just how God intends for us to treat ladies. In 1 Peter 3:7 wives are referred to as the "weaker vessel". This does not mean women are of lesser value or can't do the things men can do. It is more of a reference to how special and unique they are compared to us lumpy, clueless men. I like to put it this way, "Women are fine China and men are paper plates!"

Before you men get all upset, allow me to explain myself. When Aimee and I got home from our honeymoon, there was a huge stack of presents waiting for us in the living room of our small condo. I was pumped thinking about all the possibilities these wrapped boxes could hold. I had visions of power tools and guy gear dancing through my head. It was going to be like Christmas in July! Imagine my disappointment as present after present was opened only to discover each gift was the pieces to a China dish set Aimee had picked out and registered us for months ago. No power tools. No guy gear. Just one package at a time, a slow assembly of dishes! Within an hour we were the proud owners of a complete 8-piece set of fine China. Aimee had tears of joy, while I just had tears.

All that excitement and all that joy over fine China, and yet we have only eaten on it four times since July '92! It has been used for very special occasions and it must always be hand washed. Who would even dream of putting such special place settings in a dishwasher? You would have to be some kind of barbarian (I did this once)!

Men, our wives are to be treated like fine China. Special. Highly valued. Precious. Handled with care. The problem is we are living in a society that is treating women more like paper plates than fine China, and the next generation of boys are watching! There is an art to this . . . to being a gentleman. And it is not something that can simply be taught; it must be caught. We need to be modeling how a man should treat a lady. Let's take a look at a few time-honored ways to show our wives they are valuable to us:

> WE ARE LIVING IN A SOCIETY THAT IS TREATING WOMEN MORE LIKE PAPER PLATES THAN FINE CHINA, AND THE NEXT GENERATION OF BOYS ARE WATCHING!

Open the Door

Maybe I am just an old southerner, but I think opening the door for my wife, and really any lady, is just a basic, fundamental act of kindness and respect. It is not intended to imply women can't open their own doors, but to say you are special, highly respected, and I feel honored to serve you. I am not perfect with this art, but I do try to open the truck door for Aimee even when we are just going to the store. I would imagine the Queen of England has not opened her own door in decades. Why? Because she is royalty and is to be treated and served as such. Our wives should be treated in the same way. Like royalty, our wives are extra special, and a true treasure for us to serve.

Usher into The Room

When entering a room, church, school, office, etc., I never walk in front of Aimee. I open the door (see above paragraph) and I usher her into the room. I am so crazy proud of my bride and I want to make sure everyone knows it. To me, there is nothing worse than a guy who walks in a room alone and then a few moments later here comes his wife, following behind him like some kind of neglected puppy. This communicates I am more important and I can't wait for everyone to see me! To be honest, men, when we're with our wives, no one really cares to see us. You know as well as I do, your wife makes you look better. Usher her into the room and folks will be amazed a dude who looks like you married so well!

Stand and Greet

What if Tom Brady or Michael Jordan walked into your place of work unannounced and asked to see you? You would wipe your entire day free. You would stand, shake their hand, and get a selfie. Some of us might even have man tears from the excitement. If we would be this way with two men who we don't even know and will never see again, why not the same with our brides?

When Aimee shows up at my office, I stop everything. I wrap up a phone call. I stop a meeting. I stop taking a nap. I stand, welcome her with a smile, a hug, and if I am super lucky a kiss. I realize there may be exceptions to this at times with your work, but make sure those exceptions are rare. When we stop everything to greet her, it says "No matter what I have going on, there is still nothing as important as seeing you!"

Going for a Walk

This may sound stupid, but when Aimee and I go for walks in our neighborhood, I always walk closest to the road. In other words, I keep myself between her and any oncoming traffic. The reality is if a car goes out of control and up on the sidewalk, we are probably both goners, but it is just a simple action that says, "I am here to protect you. I will literally put my body between you and an oncoming car." Now sometimes we have been arguing while on a walk and I have gotten a little nervous she was going to push me into said oncoming car!

In a similar way, whether we are at home or traveling and staying in a hotel, I sleep closest to the door. Again, it just says I love you more than my own safety, and my last act will be to either save you or to die trying.

Kings and Queens

I mentioned earlier we should treat our wives like royalty, but let's unpack it a little further. Since my three girls were old enough to understand, I have told them they are daddy's princesses. I have tried to model for them in a way that sets the standard for what they are to look for in a man one day. I am very clear I am not perfect, but I know they are looking to me for how a man should act and how a man should treat a woman. So for those reasons I strive to live and love their momma well. This puts a lot of pressure on me, but it also provides a lot of accountability for me. I don't want my girls looking for love in all the wrong places. I want them to see how a man should cherish, respect and greatly value a lady. Princesses are in training to be queens one day and a queen should never settle for anything less than the best in the man they marry.

Even though my girls know they are my princesses, I also make it very clear momma is the queen! Let me explain what this means. If we are all in the car heading to get dinner and the princesses want Sonic, but the queen wants Chick-fil-a, then guess what? We are going to Chick-fil-a. The princesses are very special, but they are not the queen. When my girls were younger and I was leaving for work, they would be the first ones I would kiss goodbye and momma would be the last . . . and when I got home from work, momma was the first one I kissed and then my girls. Once again, it seems like a little thing, but it models for my girls that momma is the last and first one I want to see as I leave and return home. Placing a priority on our marriage in front of our children will create a stronger sense of security in a world of broken homes and divorce, which they hear about from their friends at school every day.

Here's the truth, men. I am going to keep it real with you. Every one of you wants to be treated like a king at home and at work. The problem is few of us are treating our wives like queens and yet we are still expecting the king's treatment. Do you know the difference between a boss and a leader? A boss is the guy everyone stands around the coffee pot telling jokes about and has very little desire to follow. A leader is someone who is serving those around him/her in such a way that you believe in them, you trust them and you want to go where they are going. Are you bossing, or are you leading?

God does not call us to be the boss of our home, but the sacrificial, servant leader. The title "King" has the idea of a boss, but what if it was a servant leader? Christ is called the King of Kings. Which means, of all the kings, He is the King of them all! And yet, in His last days, He washed the feet of those closest to Him, and was then beaten and eventually crucified for those who were certainly not deserving of such sacrifice. This is the kind of king we are called to be for our wives and children. Looking to serve, not to be served. Looking to be self-sacrificing, not self-preserving. You see, men, flowers and gifts are great, but it takes more than those things to make our wives feel loved and highly-valued. It takes them feeling like they are the queen because we are leading, loving and serving, not like a king, but like **the** King of kings!

✓ Action Point

Do you treat the waitress at Waffle House nicer than you do your own wife? Be honest with yourself! If you think you are the king, then when is the last time you treated your wife like a queen?

ALLOW THE MAN INSIDE OF YOU TO STAND UP AND THE BOY TO SIT DOWN.

Take your wife to dinner and apologize for taking her for-granted, for not opening doors, devaluing her opinion and treating her more like a maid than royalty. This is a varsity challenge, but you are far enough into this book for the man inside of you to stand up and the boy to sit down!

▶ Romance Tip

"License and Registration, Please"
https://www.youtube.com/watch?v=jIrhdAL4Ebw

Chapter 6

DELIVERY OPTIONS

Curt

WOW! LB, that was strong! Let me stop clapping, pause for just a second, and give a little thought as to how I can top yet another one of your chapters. This one's going to require a little effort . . . you must have read a Gary Smalley book recently and not told me about it. For our readers, though, let me be clear. I'm not shocked at all by the ideas and concepts Lance just shared – I've seen him in action for two decades, and he really does practice what he preaches. I am, however, amazed at how clearly he articulated all of that. Guys, please review some of those simple chivalric gestures. You can literally start doing those things today!

It's funny, Lance said at the beginning of the previous chapter sometimes "the delivery is the issue." Because, when I was thinking about one of the many things I've learned in over 20 years with Emily, it's the idea that the real romance is in the delivery – far more than it is in the actual gift given or words spoken. Promise me you won't skip the rest of Lance's chapters to read about my wedding in Chapter 11, but when you get there, it will be a great example of what I'm talking about in terms of delivery. Lance got married, most of you men reading this book got married, we basically all went through a similar ceremony, and we all exchanged some kind of vows. But, fellas, I delivered on this one!!! Just wait . . .

> **Bonus Section:** This is too good to pass up. My wife and I are away for a long weekend, and I'm sitting at a Denny's in Indiana, on Memorial Day having breakfast. (My wife usually gets up in time to join me for lunch . . . her ideal vacation day). I've been sitting here awhile, just drinking coffee and working on this book. My waitress, Ms. Lynn, on her last trip out to the patio to check on me, said, "You're working too hard. This is Memorial Day." I told her I'm not working hard at all, I'm having a blast writing a book. She was intrigued and asked me what it was about, so I told her it was going to be called, Love Your Wife. She laughed and then said, "Maybe I should get it for my husband." Want to know what happened next? She laughed again and said, "I'm just kidding. My husband really loves me." And she meant it – I could tell! As my breakfast got cold, she spent the next five minutes telling me exactly how her husband loves her. She was amazing – this lady went on and on, example after example. It was awesome!! It does make you wonder, though, doesn't it? If your wife stumbled into the same conversation with a stranger who was writing a book by that title, would her love cup be so overflowing with your love for her that she just couldn't pass up the opportunity to talk about it?

Thank you, Ms. Lynn . . . what a great illustration for us as we try to be the husbands our wives long for us to be.

All right now, back to "the delivery" .... I'm going to share a personal story about extremely poor delivery, and we'll walk through it together. I imagine you've got a few similar stories of your own.

So, not too long ago, 19 years into marriage, Emily and I had scheduled a three-night getaway at one of our favorite resorts. That's right ... you're thinking the same thing I was thinking: "Three straight nights, perhaps afternoons, and doubtful (yet not out of the realm of possibility) morning hotel sex! If that's a new term for you, "hotel sex" typically equates to "great sex"! Not that all sex with your wife isn't somewhere on the scale of great, but here are the very important factors related to hotel sex – especially for a woman:

- She walks into a room where the bed is made, the sheets are clean and tucked in tightly. The towels are fresh. The bathroom is spotless. And she didn't have to lift a finger for any of it!
- There's a pool waiting outside within walking distance.
- There's room service if she wants it.
- There's a TV on which she gets to watch what she wants to watch ... uninterrupted.
- There are no kids clamoring for her attention!
- And she hopefully has a husband who lets her fully enjoy all of this without any pressure to meet his needs morning, afternoon, and evening. This is where it all went south for me!

Now, I have to tell you a little bit about Emily to help you fully appreciate this story. First of all, she is a people pleaser. She lives under a lot of self-induced pressure because she does not want to disappoint anyone. This is a tall order for a wife and a mother. You just can't please everybody all of the time. And so, when we get out of town together, part of the vacation experience for her is not feeling like she has to please anybody or "be on," as she calls it. A true break for her, and I do get this, is being out from under the inherent responsibilities of being a present and intentional mother and wife. A tall order, for sure!

And secondly, my wife has an affectionate heart, but she is not a physically affectionate person. Lance and I have a buddy who jokes that his wife can't even spell the word "affection". I wouldn't go that far with Emily, but she's the first to admit it's just not how she is wired. She did not grow up receiving affection from her father, and she has a lot of fear and insecurity related to rejection. So, consequently, she avoids being vulnerable. Not a huge shocker there . . . most, if not all of us, avoid things and situations that make us feel a greater exposure to potential pain or rejection. But for me (a guy whose two dominant love languages are words of affirmation and physical touch), being married to a woman who struggles with compliments and rarely initiates anything in the realm of affection, it's easy to get frustrated and feel neglected when I'm focused on the "Big I"!

Can I Take that Back?

Well, this was one of those times. It had been quite a few days since there had been any intimacy at all – I'm not talking about sex; I'm talking about basic physical contact of any kind. Emily was laying by the pool at this resort enjoying a live DJ, a pool boy who met every hunger and thirst before she knew she had it, and a partly sunny, high 70's, truly perfect spring day.

Out comes her husband (me) from a longer than anticipated work-related conference call that was too much of a reminder there was life going on outside of this fabulous resort. I'm looking at my wife in her bathing suit – tan skin, slightly glistening from the sunscreen, shades on, one leg slightly bent, cleavage that was just beckoning me, tapping her fingers to Hall & Oates. And I'm thinking to myself, I'm at this killer resort with the hottest woman on the planet, who I gave my life to, and she gave hers to me, and I'll be lucky if I even get to touch her this weekend. What a cruel joke!

Now, let me pause and tell you this is completely untrue. And I knew it was untrue. But I was frustrated, in less than a good mood, and instead of leaning down closely to her ear and whispering something like, "Good God you are beautiful! I'm the envy of every man at this pool. I'm going to let you enjoy the sun for a while, but just know I've got a pretty amazing plan later that includes you, me, and everything you're wearing right now except for that bathing suit." Hmmm . . . I wonder how she would have responded to that! Actually, I don't have to wonder, she would have given me that grin only she can give me looking over the rim of her sunglasses, and she would have said something like, "Really? I can't wait!" Emily's good like that – she really is. Occasionally, I might get an eyeroll instead, but it's a flirty "I know what you want, big boy" kind of eyeroll.

But no, I couldn't muster something that would have fanned the flame for the rest of the weekend. Instead, I asked in a very unloving, sarcastic and accusatory tone, "Do you think you could touch me sometime in the next 12 hours?!" Dead silence followed. I think even the DJ stopped the music and everyone looked our way. She looked over at me sitting like a pouty baby on my pool chair, adjusted her shades, and turned her head back the other way, I'm sure trying to forget I existed.

Man, I was wishing with everything in me I could hit rewind. How do you recover from something like that? And, this was day one of four. Cuss! I'm an idiot!! I apologized quickly, tried to excuse it away, said it came out wrong, and everything else I could think of that was not only true, but also held some hope of salvaging our weekend. You guessed it – the damage was done.

You have every right to be thinking, "Curt, are you really writing a chapter on 'delivery'? No thanks. I'll get my counsel elsewhere." I don't blame you. I blew it, and I knew it! So, what now?

I gave her some appropriate space to cool off, but I didn't want her to have too much freedom with her thoughts because I knew it would have taken her right off the cliff and we wouldn't even talk the rest of the weekend. So, I apologized again and told her to enjoy the pool. I went to work out and told her I would just see her later when she got up to the room. Dead silence, again. Not surprising.

A Sincere Pursuit

I called her later to see what she was thinking about for dinner, and she informed me her plan was to just stay in the room for the night and probably watch TV. She freed me up to do what I wanted to do. Ouch! Now, I will tell you, there was a day in our marriage where I would have foolishly played along and said something like, "Okay, then, if you're asleep when I come in, I'll just see you in the morning." Thankfully, I have actually learned from a few of my mistakes.

Instead, I said, "I want to be with you. That's the entire reason I booked this weekend for us. I'm going to come up and talk for a few minutes just so you can hear my heart." And that's what I did. I took the elevator up to our room and shared honestly, but kindly, how difficult it is for me when we go long periods of time without any intimacy or affection. I start to feel isolated, unloved, and really vulnerable. I don't like it, and I don't handle it well. This wasn't news to her. We've had this conversation probably over 100 times in our marriage. But man, I really mishandled my approach this time. In our conversation, she did say that I need to tell her when I'm feeling that way and that I have every right to tell her when I'm feeling that way, but there's a right way and a wrong way to do it. So true!

She wasn't completely over the hurt feelings after our conversation, but she was far enough along to agree to going out for dinner and catching some live music. I worked hard all evening to genuinely care for her heart and assure her I am not the beast I can appear to be sometimes. Things worked out fine and we ended up having a great weekend together. But, had I been passive, stayed in my woundedness, and not pursued my wife's forgiveness and her heart, we could have gone a long way in the wrong direction. We used to do that . . . not anymore! Life is too short to be miserable.

> HAD I BEEN PASSIVE, STAYED IN MY WOUNDEDNESS, AND NOT PURSUED MY WIFE'S FORGIVENESS AND HER HEART, WE COULD HAVE GONE A LONG WAY IN THE WRONG DIRECTION.

So, what does that story have to do with delivery? Even the wrong or less than ideal package, if it is delivered in the right way, is palatable. Proverbs 16:24 (NIV) says, "Gracious words are a honeycomb, sweet to the soul and healing to the bones."

Think about how you approached disagreements or difficult topics when you were dating. My guess is you contemplated your approach and then did a lot of listening, really trying to understand your partner's point of view. And when you expressed your thoughts and feelings, you did so with thoughtfulness, caution and tenderness – weighing your words carefully so as not to even come close to bruising something so tender as your mate. That may sound dramatic, but I bet I'm right. You handled her with care at one point. As Lance referenced, "like fine china." So did I. I would have never made a comment like, "Do you think you could touch me sometime in the next 12 hours?" Even if I thought it, I would have never said it . . . never!

So, this is a getting back to the basics. We cannot allow "all of the water under the bridge" in our marriage to be an excuse for the way

WE CANNOT ALLOW "ALL OF THE WATER UNDER THE BRIDGE" IN OUR MARRIAGE TO BE AN EXCUSE FOR THE WAY WE SPEAK TO OR TREAT OUR WIVES.

we speak to or treat our wives. We have to man up and continue to exercise the chivalry Lance was talking about in the previous chapter. Woo your wife. Be creative in the ways you communicate your love to her. Handle and deliver with care.

If you're scratching your head, wondering what in the world I'm talking about, I'll give you an example of a pretty generic romantic gesture, but delivered in a few different ways.

Let's take, for instance, a dozen roses:

Delivery #1

It's Valentine's Day. Your calendar reminds you this is a day when you are supposed to celebrate love. So, you call and order your wife a dozen red roses in a vase for $39.99. The person taking the order asks you what you want to write on the card and she takes dictation as you say, "Happy Valentine's Day."

Delivery #2

It's the week before Valentine's Day. You go to your local florist, buy a dozen red roses arranged in a vase with Baby's Breath, you stop by the store to get a nice card for "My Wife", you sign it, and you give it to her when you get home. She says, "It's not Valentine's Day yet." And you say, "I know, but I couldn't wait that long to tell you how much I love you!"

Delivery #3

It's nowhere near Valentine's Day. You go by the local florist and order 11 roses in one color, and a single rose in your wife's favorite color. You ask the florist to arrange the roses with baby's breath, and some other complimentary flowers that point to the one favorite colored rose in the middle of the bouquet. You get some really nice stationary and you handwrite a note to your wife, telling her how lucky you are to have found her, that she is the most wonderful woman in the world, and that in every crowd there's always one who stands out, and she has always been the one. You take these to your wife's favorite restaurant and give them to the manager. You ask him to bring them out with the appetizer when you and your wife have dinner there tonight. When your wife recovers from the shock of getting these roses delivered out of nowhere, you take the note you've written to her out of your jacket pocket and you read it to her, occasionally looking into her eyes so she knows how much you mean every single word.

In each of those scenarios, the core gift is a dozen roses. The real difference is in the delivery. Let's work on our delivery guys!

✔ Action Point

Do something creative this week with flowers for your wife. If your wife doesn't like flowers, do it with candy. If she doesn't like candy, do it with something she does like . . . candles, scented lotions, food, etc. You are made in the image of a creative God. You have what it takes! Get creative and have some fun loving your wife.

▶ Romance Tip

"Suitcase Surprise"

https://www.youtube.com/watch?v=Nz0yfT8D5I8

Chapter 7

PUT YOUR CLOTHES
BACK ON!

Lance

Curt, you think you can deliver? The Domino's pizza guy has a better delivery than you! I hope we can somehow get these guys to keep reading. I am trying my best to salvage this whole book right now. I guess I better "deliver" with this chapter! To be honest, men, this chapter coming up was a tough one to write. There are a lot of things I have not done well, but what I am about to share is a time I am most ashamed of...

Is it possible to make Hawaii feel like hell? It is the paradise state. I have never heard anyone say, "We didn't like Hawaii. It just felt too perfect for us." No one says that! And yet somehow, I made our one and, so far, only trip to Hawaii anything but paradise for Aimee.

It was our 10-year anniversary and I had been saving for the previous five years to surprise her with a trip to Maui! I thought this was going to be like a second honeymoon for us. Which meant sun, fun, food and some special alone time back in the room every night...just like our first honeymoon, right? And this is where things started to come unraveled. Disappointment occurs when expectations go unmet. The problem in marriage is we don't always do a good job of expressing our expectations, but have no problem expressing our disappointment when the unsaid expectations go unmet. Did that last sentence make any sense? I expected it to, but now I am not sure and feel disappointed! You see, I had convinced myself when Aimee found

DISAPPOINTMENT OCCURS WHEN EXPECTATIONS GO UNMET.

out how long I had saved and how hard I had worked to surprise her with this trip . . . well, I would probably need pepper spray to keep her off of me! And this hope became an expectation which set me up for disappointment. All my well-intentioned work and plans to make this all about Aimee quickly dissolved down to being about me.

It was day four of our trip and I was in the room having a pity party, wondering how in the world I could have such a selfish wife. The way I saw it . . . I did all this planning and spent all this money so she could go on her dream trip to paradise! Paradise?! That's a joke! All I wanted in return was a little special attention, just some love and affection from my wife of 10 years! Good grief, is that too much to ask after all I did for her?! Unmet expectations . . . let me introduce you to disappointment. The problem is disappointment leads to frustrations, and frustrations lead to anger or, in my case, pouting in the room.

Meanwhile, as I am contemplating my entire existence up in the room, Aimee was walking on the beach. In Maui. Crying. Alone! She had dreamed of going to Hawaii since she was a little girl, and I had taken her dream and made it a nightmare. Don't get me wrong, it wasn't all bad, the first few days went great. The hotel was awesome.

The view from our room was amazing. It was whale season, and we sat on our balcony and watched humpback whales all afternoon. It truly was paradise. Then things began to change. Aimee wanted to do more sight-seeing, talking and "investing" in our relationship. And, instead of being present mentally and emotionally with my wife, I chose to plan and even manipulate how we could get back to the room for some "us" time. So, because of me, our individual expectations for the trip did not sync and paradise quickly became prison.

Can she trust you?

Aimee and I both agreed on one thing after our trip to paradise. Her husband could not be trusted. It is hard for me to even type those words, but they are true ... I could not be trusted. She could trust me to be faithful. She could trust me to be home when I said I would. She could trust me to love our kids and be the best dad I knew how. But she could no longer trust I loved her for her heart and for her as a person. As she put it, "I feel like you only love me for sex, and our marriage has to be based on more than just that!" My wife has always been subtle like a gun!

Of course, she was right. Our marriage couldn't be just based on sex, but I did have the passing thought, "Well, we could at least give it a shot for a few weeks and see if a marriage could thrive based solely on sex." Who knows? Maybe I was on to something. Maybe we could have been marriage pioneers! Don't roll your judgmental eyes at me ... like you have never thought this? Let's be honest, men, when we got married, back in our twenties, we thought one of the perks of marriage was we were going to have sex every night, maybe even morning and night some days!

As I shared earlier, life sets in quickly, and it did for us right after the honeymoon. We had jobs, deadlines, mortgage payments, car payments, and we haven't even gotten to having kids yet! All of this reality makes it hard to find quality time together. And when there is time, our wives don't always have the energy for sex, which is difficult for us to understand because we cannot think of a scenario where we would ever be too tired ... ICU? Maybe. Coma? Perhaps. But some of us would still find a way!

All of this sets up an issue in our marriages. Our wives feel like they are prisoners in their own bedrooms. They come to bed each night wondering if he is going to hit on me. Dreading the thought of having to turn him down because she is too tired. Knowing he would never understand her feeling disconnected emotionally because they haven't had a conversation about something other than work, weather or the kids in weeks. Hear this, men ... *Our wives need to feel close to us before they can be intimate with us.*

After 25+ years of marriage and doing a whole lot of marriage counseling, I truly believe trust is the most important virtue in a marriage relationship. Not love. We have made love more of a feeling than a virtue. We fall in love and we fall out of love, but you can't fall in to trust and fall out of trust. Trust is something that is earned over time and can be lost in a moment. My moment was on our anniversary trip. I made Aimee feel cheap, not cherished. Instead of deepening our relationship and building trust, I just wanted passion. It seems to work in the movies, but this is the real world. And in the real-world, passion is for a moment and trust is for a lifetime.

OUR WIVES NEED TO FEEL CLOSE TO US BEFORE THEY CAN BE INTIMATE WITH US.

So, what did I do to rebuild trust in the bedroom? Honestly, I am still working on it even to this day. Does that discourage you? Don't let it! I'm going to keep repeating this until you get it ... Trust is built over a lifetime, but lost in a moment. You know how I started building back the trust? By trusting Aimee. What? Yeah, I had to start trusting her. You see, I found out there were two reasons why I would "hit on" her every night at bedtime: 1) I thought that was what men were supposed to do. I grew up around men who were always hitting on women, even ones who weren't their wives. So, I just thought that was part of being a man ... to expect sex all the time, and 2) I was worried if I didn't bring up sex regularly, then Aimee might go weeks, even months, without ever thinking about it. I thought it was my duty to remind her, to make sure her priorities were in order and to keep her focused on what was most important ... my needs! It turns out I didn't trust her either, and that was why sex had become such an issue in our marriage. You see, trust invades every area of our relationship, and the depth of trust will determine the quality of our marriages.

> **TRUST INVADES EVERY AREA OF OUR RELATIONSHIP, AND THE DEPTH OF TRUST WILL DETERMINE THE QUALITY OF OUR MARRIAGES.**

You Know How to Lust, But Do You Know How to Trust?

Do you have a life verse? I know some guys who have had several life verses over the years based on their specific season of life, but for me I have had just one:

> *Trust in the Lord with all your heart,*
> *and do not rely on your own understanding;*
> *think about Him in all your ways,*
> *and He will guide you on the right paths.*
> *Proverbs 3:5-6 (HCSB)*

That first line speaks to trust. It is interesting God doesn't say here to trust Him with all our abilities, all our money, all our skills or even all our knowledge. He tells us to trust Him with all our heart. Coaches I have worked with know the most important thing is an athlete's heart. Their heart determines how hard they will work, for sure, but more importantly, when an athlete gives their heart over to the program and to the coach, then everything else will follow. His or her skills will follow their heart. His or her work ethic will follow their heart. His or her abilities will follow their heart. So, if a coach can win over the heart of an athlete, then the sky is the limit as to what they can do as an individual and how they can contribute to the team. Similarly, God knows if we will trust Him with all our heart, then everything else about us will follow Him as well.

There is an old saying, "At the heart of any issue is a heart issue." If trust has been broken in your marriage, then you have to go after the heart. I realized my heart was not in the right condition to love Aimee well. My heart was not solely focused on her needs and well-being, but about my needs, wants and expectations. Even deeper, my heart was not solely focused on Christ. I had created an idol in my heart of lust and sex. Wait, is lust wrong if you are lusting for your wife? Yes, if it forms an idol in your heart that takes your focus away from Christ. Don't miss my point here, men: my heart and my focus were the problem, not the sex. Inside a Christ-centered marriage, sex is a great thing. It is a wonderful gift God gave a husband and wife to enjoy for procreation and recreation. But it is not to be at the expense of all other areas of the relationship. Definitely not at the expense of your wife's sense of trust in her own bedroom.

I had to do some heart surgery. I had to evaluate my priorities. I had to ask myself some tough questions about what it meant to be a Godly man . . . a man whose heart is focused on Christ and allows everything else to flow from that relationship. As I began to "trust the Lord with all my heart" and stop relying "on my own understanding" and began to "think about Him in all my ways" . . . He started "guiding me on the right paths" for myself AND for my marriage. I slowly removed the idol of sex from my heart and returned Christ to His rightful place in my heart, my life and my marriage. The idol still creeps back in from time to time, but I recognize it quickly and get back to a healthy place.

We will talk more about this later in the book, but as our trust in the Lord grows, we open the door for our wives to trust us again. I am not saying if you get your heart right and start living for Christ that your wife will immediately start trusting you again and you will live happily ever after. There may be some heart issues for her as well. It could be issues put there by how she was treated by you, or maybe it is something deeper. There could be pain from other men in her past that will cause her to doubt your sincerity. Some things can be talked out, but if there are deeper wounds needing to be addressed, you may need to take the lead and find a Christian counselor who can help you and your wife begin to walk and talk things out. Your marriage is worth it, and I am certain your bride is worth it, too!

"One Small Step for Man, One Giant Leap for Mankind"

We can put a man on the moon, but we have yet to figure out how to treat, cherish and love our wives fully the way God intended. The struggle is real, men! But I believe there are a lot of men who desire excellence in areas other than just work and play. Men who are tired of average marriages and want more. Men who are willing to go the extra mile to love their wives and their families. Men who are done asking what the price is because they are determined to pay whatever the cost!

This was me shortly after *paradise* with Aimee. I wanted to be this kind of man. I had not had anything like this modeled for me growing up, but I refused to allow that to be an excuse or a crutch. My wife deserved more. She deserved a man who trusted the Lord first and loved her with no expectations. Therefore, since Aimee and I had decided in our first year of marriage to never even mention the word divorce, I knew I had one of two options at this point . . . 1) murder, or 2) get to work on me and my heart in hopes Aimee would trust me again and believe I loved her for more than just her body. This meant cuddling with her before going to sleep without making sexual comments or innuendos. Doing something called "non-sexual touch," which I thought was some kind of oxymoron like jumbo shrimp, but it turns out it is holding hands on a walk or rubbing her feet while watching TV (who knew?)! The key was me doing these things for the right reasons and with the right motives. My heart had to be in a different place, and my focus had to be on her, not me.

However, this is not a small step for us, men . . . it is a huge leap. A leap of faith. What if you do heart surgery and start living in a new way, but she does not respond? Can you stay the course? We have to take a leap that says, "I am going to love her unconditionally even if she loves me with boundaries . . . I am going to genuinely trust her even if she doubts my sincerity". This is when it gets real, guys. This is when we have to go where few men dare to go . . . to a place called vulnerability. Vulnerability is possibly the scariest place for all men, but it is also where trust is forged and marriages go from mediocre to off the chart amazing! It is a place where we feel exposed and weak, but where we will find the most strength to love our wives well.

Curt will talk more about vulnerability in the next chapter, but for now, I'm encouraging you to take the leap. All of mankind is counting on you ... okay, maybe just your family is counting on you, but either way it is a big deal!

✔ Action Points

Do you feel you should be having more sex each week? (Every husband always says, "YES" to this question.) What if husbands quit expecting sex from their wives and started demanding more romance from themselves? Could you love and romance your wife with no hidden agenda . . . no ulterior motive? Just love her for who she is, not what she can do for you.

This week find time each day to:

- Sit on the couch holding hands or cuddled up watching a show.
- Let her lay her head on your chest before bed or when you first wake up and take a moment to tell her five non-physical things that make her special to you.
- Don't just kiss her goodbye on the way out the door to work, but pause, set your briefcase down and give her a big bear hug and wait until she starts to pull away . . . she might even relax and lay her head on your shoulder for a moment.

Disclaimer: none of these are intended to lead to sex, and you have to do them with NO expectation. Be a giver, not a taker!

▶ Romance Tip

"Bedroom Surprise"

*https://www.youtube.com/
watch?v=X8aTNSO-few&t=29s*

Chapter 8

EXPOSING YOURSELF:
BEING VULNERABLE
AND MAINTAINING
YOUR MANHOOD

Curt

That's a great set up, Lance. Thanks for your vulnerability! Lance and I are writing this book because of what we've learned from our own mistakes and experiences, but also what we've learned from counseling and coaching hundreds and hundreds of men in the past three decades.

We're going to take a pretty deep dive in this chapter, but I want you to know it is a scary adventure worth taking. And, even though you may feel alone, trust me . . . you are not alone! I've been here before. I'm fearful every single time. Literally, without exception – but it is worth the trip!

Let's start with this question: "Where are you?"

"Uh, let's see, Curt. I'm sitting in a chair, reading a book. Why do you ask?"

I ask because this is a life-changing question. I told you we're going deep, and we're not going to waste any time, so go ahead and put on your fins, your tank, your snorkel, and your mask. Here we go . . .

Did you know this was the first question God ever asked a man? "And God said to Adam, 'Where are you?'" Just to give you a little background, in Genesis chapters one and two we see Creation unfold by the spoken word of God. Everything came into existence: the entire solar system and outer space, the earth, the seas, the various lights in the sky, the vegetation, the birds of the sky, the creatures of the sea, and all of the land animals. As His final act of this magnificent Creation, he forms Man (male and female). He doesn't speak man into existence like He did the rest of Creation; He forms him with his own hands. And then He uses His own breath and breathes life into Mankind. Do you sense the special connection between God and man already? It was very personal between God and Adam and Eve. He formed them. He breathed life into them. And He spoke *with* them. He was a conversational, relational God. This is so crazy cool! This is the same God, by the way, who formed you and breathed life into you. See Psalm 139.

Everything was perfect! God, and Adam, and Eve, in the midst of this beautiful Creation, were together. Together. At peace. Unified. In relationship with one another. Loving. Open in communication. Accepted. Fearless.

I'll be honest with you – even as I write those words, I find myself a little breathless. That's a profound paragraph that bears repeating:

Everything was perfect!
God, and Adam, and Eve,
in the midst of this beautiful Creation, were together.
Together. At peace. Unified.
In relationship with one another.
Loving.
Open in communication.
Accepted.
Fearless.

Let that sink in for a second. This was God's perfect plan for us. To have this kind of relationship with Him and to have it with each other.

A New Reality

So, what happened? There have been thousands of books written to answer that question, and since the purpose of this particular book is something entirely different, I'm going to sum it up for you pretty simply:

God gave Adam and Eve the ability to choose, and they chose to do what they wanted to do instead of what God told them to do. And consequently, this broke the perfect relationship and fellowship that existed prior to their self-serving choice.

This is where it gets personal. Do you know what Adam and Eve did when they realized they had disobeyed God? Two things. And this is so universally known even after several thousand years, I bet you already know what they did – even if you're not a Bible scholar.

First, they covered themselves with fig leaves to cover the shame and nakedness they were feeling for the first time. And second, they hid themselves from God because they were afraid. Oh man. Can we please rewind the tape a few paragraphs? It is no longer:

> ... *Together. At peace. Unified.*
> *In relationship with one another.*
> *Loving.*
> *Open in communication.*
> *Accepted.*
> *Fearless.*

Not even close. There is a very clear disconnect and separation. It is absolutely heartbreaking! The new reality is:

> *Alone. Fearful. Isolated.*
> *Relationship is broken.*
> *Judged.*
> *Quiet and shut down.*
> *Rejected.*
> *Afraid.*

Are you angry when you read that? Sad when you read that? I am. How could this happen?

Now, before we get too far down the road of, "How could God let this happen?" or "Who is God to judge or call something sin when He's the One who gave them the choice in the first place," let's look at God's response to what just happened. Better yet, before we do that, let's look at what His response could have been. He could have rolled them up like a spit wad in between his thumb and forefinger and flicked them into oblivion. He could have rubbed them out like a cigarette back into the dust out of which they were created. He could have tortured them, yelled at them, beat them, killed them, and started over with a better model. He could have ignored them, left them to fend for themselves and gone and created another world. His options were endless. Truly, endless. He's God.

But the God of the universe, who has ALL of the rights and ALL of the power, and who has just been rejected by the two people who He lovingly created, does something very curious and, quite honestly, very humbling. He comes to them. He initiates relationship even though He was the One who was offended. And He asks the question, "Where are you?"

Finding Freedom

I want to share with you why I think this is so profound. First of all, I hope we can agree God wasn't asking because He wasn't sure where Adam was. He knew exactly where he was. He could have given you the GPS coordinates, Adam's heartrate, blood pressure, red and white blood cell count, the type of bush he was hiding behind, and every single thought racing through Adam's mind as he heard God approaching. God is God. He knows it all. So, there is obviously more behind this question than God seeking information. God asks questions for our benefit, not for His.

What then, would be the benefit in Adam answering this question? I'll give it to you in one word and then we'll unpack it. Any idea what the word is? It's *freedom*. God wants Adam to be free. Prior to disobeying God, Adam and Eve were completely free. That's the way God intended for us to live and enjoy life. "They were naked and they felt no shame." God is asking the question in order to lead Adam back into freedom. In the New Testament, we see this stated for the

Believer in Jesus. Galatians 5:1 (NIV) says, "It is for freedom that Christ has set us free. Stand firm, then, and do not let yourselves be burdened again by a yoke of slavery."

We've all experienced the feelings associated with trying to hide, deceive, or cover something up. There is a total absence of peace. We're constantly looking over our shoulder, weighing our words so we don't reveal anything we don't want to, trying to figure out whether or not somebody actually knows what we did. It's miserable. I've worked in prisons for years, and this concept of freedom is something that resonates for obvious reasons. Guys who are incarcerated will readily admit they often feel freer in prison than they have felt their entire lives. When they are on the streets running from the police, deceiving and lying to family members, lawyers and judges, trying to hide evidence, and appear to be something they are not, they are living in absolute bondage. Once the truth comes to light and there is full confession, it's as if the weight of the world has come off of their shoulders. There's nothing left to hide. Even behind bars they at least have peace of mind . . . and yes, freedom.

> **WE'VE ALL EXPERIENCED THE FEELINGS ASSOCIATED WITH TRYING TO HIDE, DECEIVE, OR COVER SOMETHING UP. THERE IS A TOTAL ABSENCE OF PEACE.**

I hope you can sense the heart of God in this question. He is giving Adam an opportunity to confess and find freedom, again. Come clean, Adam. Be free.

God is asking you and me this same question right now. "Where are you, Curt? Come clean." Every time we make choices for our own selfish desires instead of choices that honor His plan and purpose for our lives, we should learn to hear this question. We can ignore Him, keep hiding, run the other way, or a multitude of other things you and

I have mastered, but we will not be free. It may feel like freedom for a period of time. Some of us have lived in bondage for so long it feels normal. But it's not true freedom. Ultimately, in our relationship with God and with others, we are . . .

> *Alone. Fearful. Isolated.*
> *Relationship is broken.*
> *Judged.*
> *Quiet and shut down.*
> *Rejected.*
> *Afraid.*

When a circus acquires a baby elephant, they tie him with a short rope to a small stake in the ground. The young elephant is not strong enough to pull the stake out and free himself, so he quits trying. Eventually, even though the elephant has grown big and strong and is completely capable of freedom, he is so accustomed to the boundaries of the rope and his inability to break free, that he lives his life in unnecessary bondage. Is that you?

> **SOME OF US HAVE LIVED IN BONDAGE FOR SO LONG IT FEELS NORMAL.**

If your "secret life" were laid bare before your wife, your kids, the world, and God . . . which paragraph would define you?

> *Alone. Fearful. Isolated.*
> *Relationship is broken.*
> *Judged.*
> *Quiet and shut down.*
> *Rejected.*
> *Afraid.*

Or,

Together. At peace. Unified.
In relationship with one another.
Loving.
Open in communication.
Accepted.
Fearless.

God was calling Adam to confession and repentance. He's calling you and me to the same thing. To live in the true freedom and authentic shameless relationship in which we were designed to live.

Freedom is Compelling and Contagious

"Curt, what does this have to do with loving my wife?" you ask. Great question! Here's the answer. If you and I are not living "Together, at peace, unified, in loving relationship with open communication, feeling accepted and fearless" with God, there is zero chance we are going to be able to lead our wives into this kind of relationship with Him, and eventually, prayerfully with us. And you, friend, are called to live in freedom and lead your wife into it, as well.

Deep water, men. I know it. This is deep water. Are you afraid? This is unknown territory for most men, so we avoid it at all cost. But, can you sense the adventure? Aren't you curious if God can really give you that kind of freedom and peace? Wouldn't you love to know what it's like to be literally and figuratively naked in front of your wife and feel no shame? Not because you're perfect, but because you have confessed your imperfection. You have owned it. You have found forgiveness, and it has allowed you to extend the same acceptance and forgiveness to your wife for her imperfections.

Adam, the first man, who knew God and walked with Him was afraid. He knew what God was capable of, but he also knew the heart of God and realized God had come to him to restore relationship. God is the ultimate pursuer. The ultimate reconciler. Just like He went personally to Adam in the Garden, He came again to us in the form of a man, Jesus, so we could fully know Him. And the message has not changed. I John 1:9 (NIV) says, "If we confess our sins, He is faithful and just and will forgive us our sins and purify us from all unrighteousness." That sounds like FREEDOM!!!

So, how do you expose yourself, be vulnerable, and still keep your "man card"? Dear Reader, that is how you GET your "man card"! If you are not in an honest and vulnerable relationship with God and with your wife, you are faking it. I say that with love but with deep conviction, because I was a Fake, yes, with a capital "F", for many years. And if I'm not in constant confession and confronting my tendency to hide my nakedness and shame, I am still fully capable of hiding out in the bushes and trying to convince myself and everyone else I'm free.

> **IF YOU ARE NOT IN AN HONEST AND VULNERABLE RELATIONSHIP WITH GOD AND WITH YOUR WIFE, YOU ARE FAKING IT.**

Life is too short and far too precious to spend it in hiding and in bondage. And sadly, people living in bondage tend to lead other people into the same bondage. Free yourself, free your wife, free your children. Confess! Repent! Forgive! Lead! Change! Love!

"He who conceals his transgressions will not prosper, but he who confesses and forsakes them will find compassion." Proverbs 28:13 (NASB)

✔ Action Point

First, spend some time alone, listening to your own heart. What fears, insecurities and sins haunt you? Confess them to God. Come clean. He already knows. He is patiently waiting for you to acknowledge it and receive the freedom He has for you.

Secondly, share your newfound freedom with your wife. Tell her what you learned from this chapter and that, as scary as it is, you would love to learn what it means to live in freedom together.

You can do this! Take the plunge . . .

▶ Romance Tip

 **"No Pane, No Gain"**

https://www.youtube.com/watch?v=H1BtOROBibg

Chapter 9

THREE D'S THAT WILL KEEP YOU FROM THE BIG D

Lance

I have known Curt for 25 years and there are times I wish he would be a little less vulnerable! Have you ever heard of oversharing?! Lol! Seriously, this is a big time struggle for men and a great challenge from Curt. Let's head back into the locker room for some halftime adjustments. This chapter coming up has some things in it that have taken my marriage from average to amazing...

Aimee and I come from two very different families. Her parents, grandparents, aunts and uncles have all stayed married to the same person for the long haul. Her family tree looks like an oak tree with clear strong branches and leaves. My family has a history of affairs and divorces all up and down the tree. We have branches, leaves, stumps and maybe even a full-blown forest fire in there somewhere! For this reason, Aimee's folks were a little apprehensive when we started talking about marriage. In fact, they told Aimee they were not sure if I was the right fit for her because I had not seen commitment within marriage modeled anywhere in my life.

The truth is the divorce rate in our country is no respecter of race, income or even beliefs. Actually, the numbers on divorce within the church are almost identical to those couples not in a faith community. The primary reason for couples calling it quits is we are more of a reactive culture than we are a proactive culture. We have the approach of survival in our marriages instead of looking for ways to thrive in our marriages. The difficulty with being proactive in our marriages is it requires more effort, more intentionality, more creativity and more planning on our part as men.

WE HAVE THE APPROACH OF SURVIVAL IN OUR MARRIAGES INSTEAD OF LOOKING FOR WAYS TO THRIVE IN OUR MARRIAGES.

As I have already shared, Aimee and I have had our share of struggles. Thankfully we made a pact to never, ever, under any circumstances use the word divorce in our marriage. I am happy to say we have both kept our word by not saying that word. Now, don't let me paint too pretty a picture here . . . I think Aimee has used words like murder, dufus, grow up and idiot more than once! My precious angel has a way with words. Seriously, even though we have agreed to not say "divorce", we have certainly said some other things we have regretted.

Unfortunately, the growing trend in today's marriages is you don't even have to be going through tough times for divorce to be an option. We now start considering divorce when the marriage has become inconvenient or just not fun anymore or "I am not happy and I know God wants me to be happy". This is more of the reactive model. We make decisions based on our feelings and our emotions. Let me ask you something, men: when was the last time you made a big decision at your workplace based on your emotions? And yet, many men have walked out on their wives and children simply because they "lost that loving feelin'". Emotions and feelings will lie to us and can't be trusted when our families are on the line!

This will sound harsh, but God is more concerned with our obedience than our happiness. The covenant of marriage and our willingness to battle through the hard times with our wives is what God calls us to do as men. Happiness comes and goes based on emotions and external circumstances. It is elusive and temporary. If we gauge our marriage on emotions and happiness, this will send us on a roller coaster ride of ups and downs that will leave us in real trouble. I am not saying we will never be happy in our marriages, or we shouldn't strive for happiness. However, if our commitment to our marriage is going to be determined by whether we are happy 24/7, then this is not a stable foundation for any relationship.

> **GOD IS MORE CONCERNED WITH OUR OBEDIENCE THAN OUR HAPPINESS.**

There is another option. Although happiness is hard to maintain, joy is something we can have every day. Unlike happiness, joy's source is internal and is fed by hope! Aimee and I have not always been happy in our marriage. The outside stresses of bills, extended family, work and parenting all can steal happiness. However, we have always had a joy in our marriage. Because of our commitment to never say the "D" word and our desire to obey God above our own feelings, we have had a hope and joy that we can, and will, get through whatever the world throws at us . . . together!

So, what are some practical, or should I say proactive, ways to avoid the "Big D"? I was about to answer that, so it's amazing you asked! These are not things that will fix a marriage in crisis, but they are things to KEEP a marriage from crisis! Aimee and I have tried (not perfectly) to keep three little D's in our lives to avoid the Big D. Here we go ...

D ialogue Daily

My job requires a lot of listening, but most folks come to me for advice, not for me to just listen ... which translates to my job also requiring a lot of talking. As a man, I have usually used up most of my daily words by lunch time! In the early years of our marriage, Aimee was home all day with little kids watching Barney, Dora the Explorer and Veggie Tales. She was craving some adult conversation! Many days our two worlds collided and I failed as a husband. I just didn't have it in me to do a lot of talking and/or listening for that matter. I was selfish and not very emotionally attentive to my wife.

Does this sound familiar in your marriage? I had expectations of coming home with dinner on the table, kids bathed and in their right minds (which are really high expectations). Then once we finished dinner, Aimee would turn on Monday Night Football, hand me the remote and say, "I will be back to rub your shoulders after I do the dishes". However, her expectations were surprisingly different. She has been at home with beforementioned kids who are NOT in their right minds, which means Aimee is no longer in her right mind! She has lived in a world of dirty diapers, crayons on the walls, vacuuming cheerios off the couch and discovering that the growing smell over the past four days is an old sippy cup of milk (now more like cottage cheese) that rolled under my recliner three weeks ago! When these two worlds collided, it got ugly! As I stated earlier, one of the biggest causes of arguments is unmet expectations. And the main reason for unmet expectations is lack of communication.

So, this leads me to ask you men . . . how often do you and your bride talk during a normal day? And what does a normal day look like? Ours had become a goodbye kiss as I headed out the door, an "I'm home" kiss when I arrived home, drive-thru dinners, working on homework with kids and/or playing ball in the yard before dark. We would usually find some time to talk once the kids were asleep and we were in bed. However, this was typically post 10 p.m., and once my head hits the pillow there are NO guarantees of me remaining conscious more than 90 seconds.

Take Time to Talk

We men are so good at scheduling our time and tasks. We know what meetings we have on the horizon each week, and we are constantly preparing to attack the day. I believe there are two important meetings each day I cannot afford to miss. The truth is I can feel it on the inside when I miss one or both of these meetings! The first is my early morning, before anyone is up, time with the Lord. This is my time to read my Bible, pray for my day and my family, and even journal (I have confirmed this is not a man card violation). The second meeting I must have every day is with Aimee. At some point every day (usually in the evening) you will find Aimee and me talking about our day, the kids, and what God has for us tomorrow.

We have to be intentional for these daily dialogues to not just be about the kids or work. We want this to be about us and our lives. Not every time, but at least once a week we try to make our daily talks about anything but the kids. Not that talking about the kids is a bad thing, but one day the kids will be gone and we need to be investing in the two of us for the day when it's just the two of us! This will require us to go deeper, men. Move past the shallow water talks of weather, sports and the kids. Have you ever talked about places you want to go together? What did you think about church this past Sunday and the message? Maybe you even take time to express how you feel about each other and what she means to you. As marriages start gaining years, they start losing affection and encouragement. Take time to tell your wife why you love her today, what she specifically does each week as a mom and wife that means so much to you, and how she is still the prettiest woman you know!

Sunday Nights

Sunday nights are a great example of how we try to be intentional in our daily conversations. I am a planner and like to look at my week, check my daily schedule, and go over my task list regularly. Aimee is more of an "in the moment" kind of person. Whereas I can see things coming up, not just this next summer, but even five and ten years from now . . . Aimee doesn't really like to look past lunch at Chick-fil-a. This has caused moments where we have had something on the calendar for months and the night before, in a panic, Aimee says "Wait, that's tomorrow? I can't do that tomorrow!" This

> **AS MARRIAGES START GAINING YEARS, THEY START LOSING AFFECTION AND ENCOURAGEMENT.**

causes a less than patient response from me and usually ends with us cancelling whatever we had on the calendar for tomorrow and me on the couch!

One of the dialogue daily ideas is to take a few minutes on Sunday nights to look at the coming week. We sit in bed, each with our preferred calendar methods. I and my iPad with color coded appointments synched to all my devices and Aimee with her big, old-school notebook calendar with drawings, pictures and hearts around special days. Regardless of your method, taking the time to talk through the upcoming week with the hopes of avoiding any surprises can go a long way in avoiding unnecessary arguments due to lack of communication. These Sunday night talks also give me a chance to see where I might be able to serve and help Aimee during any given week. Like when the kids have doctors' visits on a Thursday, a day I could work from home, I can take the kids to the doctor and out for ice cream while Aimee goes to lunch with a friend! Aimee gets time with a friend and dad is a hero for getting ice cream! If we don't talk on Sunday nights, then that day becomes a ball of stress for her instead of a potential break.

D ate Weekly

Okay, so maybe you do well with "dialogue daily", but what about a weekly date night? This one has been a little tougher for Aimee and me for a few reasons. My work is very seasonal, and there are certain times of the year when my schedule is more date friendly than other times. But I must not allow my schedule to be an excuse for not making time to date my wife! She is worth whatever effort it requires to find time for a date. Plus, I *want* to go on a date with her! Remember what we have said earlier, whatever you did to win her heart is the same thing you do to keep her heart. One of the things I did to win Aimee's heart was creating a date night experience. If I want to keep her heart, then I better get to creating experiences a woman like her deserves.

The other issue we have had with weekly dates is we each define the word "date" differently based on our unspoken expectations (there are those crazy expectations again). I see a date as any time we are having a meal, don't have the kids and at some point, we hold hands. This could be a lunch near my office on a work day or dinner with another couple while our kids are at Wednesday youth church.

Aimee sees these as nice times together, but not anything that took any creativity or planning on my part. They just happened and were probably going to happen regardless. What this means is I am not going to get any points on the scoreboard of romance for these dates. Aimee's definition of a date is more detailed. It does not always mean spending money on a fancy meal downtown, but it does mean I have taken time to plan an experience. I have coordinated childcare (when our kids were little) and have planned an evening with her in mind. It could be a meal at her favorite restaurant or something way cheaper like chocolate milkshakes and a summer walk at our local park.

> **WHATEVER YOU DID TO WIN HER HEART IS THE SAME THING YOU DO TO KEEP HER HEART.**

I know what you're thinking. This seems unfair. Shouldn't anytime we have together be good enough? Sure. There have been weeks when our date was with our favorite friends to our favorite chippy-dippy (our word for Mexican food). But we as men must take the lead here and not allow our weekly dates to become routine and mundane. That is why I am always asking myself these questions:

- How can I make Aimee feel special this week?
- What is something that would make her smile?
- What is something that will require more effort than money and show more love than obligation?

It is not the weekly date that is special, but who you are with on the date that makes the date special! Winning a woman's heart is easy and boys do it every week, but keeping a woman's heart takes hard work, time and creativity, and only **men** can do that every week!

Depart Quarterly

Because I like to travel, this is the one I enjoy the most. There is something about getting away that is just good for the soul. And if it is good for one soul, then it must be twice as good for two souls! When the kids were little it was super hard for Aimee to leave them, but she also knew a short time away was what *she* needed, what *we* needed, and what *our kids* needed. We found that taking a one or two night break away from work, home and the kids actually made us better parents. Time to refresh, reenergize and reconnect helped us have the patience and energy to jump back into parenting our four amazing kids.

We have not always gotten out of town quarterly, but it is certainly a goal worth striving for. We have been blessed with friends who have offered their lake house or mountain cabin for a night, but it could be as simple as heading to the other side of the city for one or two nights away. Where you go doesn't really matter, just go!

Please Don't Kill Me!

For over 20 years I have worked closely with a college Power 5 football program. This means my falls are absolutely insane. I work a crazy number of hours, which puts a lot of stress on Aimee to hold things together at home. This was especially true when our kids were young. So, I decided to start giving her a trip at the end of each season to give her something to look forward to and, selfishly, in hopes she would not kill her husband before the end of football season! In fact, I call it the, "You made it through another football season without killing your husband trip".

Some years I saved up enough SkyMiles and hotel points for us to go Christmas shopping in Chicago. Other years we went to a cabin in the mountains, thanks to a friend. The big year was when we went to Margo Island, Florida and rode wave runners with dolphins! These were all two to four day trips I researched, saved for and booked. I told her when we were leaving and what to pack; the rest was all on me. It was my way of treating my queen like a queen. A very brief time to thank her for enduring a very long season. Because I am so distracted during the season, I made sure on these trips she was my sole focus. No emails. No calls. No texts. Just me and my girl.

Our Secret Place

Aimee and I have another place we discovered about six years into our marriage. It is classified as a bed and breakfast, but it is more like a lake resort in East Tennessee. This is our heaven on earth. This is where we go to stop going. There are some places it takes a few days to unwind, fully rest and recharge. But when we pull though the red barn entrance, we both feel like we have entered our own secret hideaway and, literally, the outside stresses melt away instantly.

So, men, we have work to do. If we don't want divorce to be a word mentioned in our marriage, then we better get to dialoguing, dating and departing. Don't wait until your marriage is in crisis, because then you are trying to survive when God has called us to thrive. Start doing these things today and be proactive in keeping crisis out of your marriage. These are not foolproof steps to a perfect marriage, but they are three great ways to invest in your wife. Be intentional, be proactive and be a man of action. Your marriage AND your wife are worth the investment!

Action Points

Ask your wife to block out an evening this week and have her bring her calendar. Tell her you are working on some ways to be a better husband and you want her help. Then, determine a night of the week that works for both of you and make it your "date night". This can be a full-blown date experience some weeks, or other weeks it may just be grabbing dinner near home with another couple.

Then, ask her to find a two to three day window in the next couple of months when the two of you can get away together. Ask her if there is somewhere she has been wanting to go? The mountains? Hiking? The beach? Get a sunburn? Or maybe it is just a staycation on the other side of the city. Let her know you just want to be with her . . . without work or kids. You want to give her your full focus and attention.

Romance Tip

 **Hotel Sex**
https://www.youtube.com/watch?v=06qNwP-zbKE

Chapter 10

BEWARE...DON'T
GET HOOKED

Curt

Thanks for the reminder, LB! The three D's ... dialogue daily, date weekly, and depart quarterly. Emily and I have worked hard through the years to get quality time together, regardless of the season of life and ages of our children. The investment has paid off! As we embark on the empty nest journey, we are excited about continuing to deepen our relationship ... we're not starting over and trying to get to know each other again. Hallelujah!

When I was a young boy, I was captivated by the mountains. My family went to Colorado every summer for a week to escape the Texas heat. The thought of hiking five miles without breaking a sweat, or actually having to wear a hoodie to stay warm in August, was enough to convince my folks to load my sister and me in the car and drive fourteen hours. I'm so thankful they did. In so many ways the Rocky Mountains have shaped my life.

Every year, we would rent a cabin on The Big Thompson River in Estes Park. The first five years of my life I was toddling around, playing in the fresh cut grass and the sand along the river, throwing rocks, feeding peanuts to chipmunks, and braving the unfamiliar chill of a river formed by snowmelt – only up to my ankles, of course. The current was strong enough a few feet off shore to send a kid downriver in a hurry, even in only two feet of water.

My dad and grandpa had both taught me how to fish at a young age, but in early elementary school I really started to develop a passion for it. In Texas, of course, it was primarily largemouth bass, crappie, and blue gill. My dad would wake me up early on a Saturday morning, we would swing by a bait shop to get a carton of worms and a couple dozen minnows, and then head to a stock pond in rural Texas where the cottonmouths rivaled anacondas. Well, maybe not, but it seemed like it at the time. We had a few close encounters, but they never thwarted our quest for taking home a full stringer of bass and crappie for dinner. And we usually did.

Every summer in Colorado, one of our first stops when we got to town was Scott's Sporting Goods. I was fascinated with some of the gear lining the walls that was unique to trout fishing. I had never had the occasion in Texas to use salmon eggs or colored marshmallows. But what really grabbed my attention was the 50 to 60 matchbox sized containers filled with a variety of hand tied flies. Even before I knew what they were, I was intrigued with their size and detail. I didn't have a clue how to use one. My dad would buy a license, we would get a map of the mountain streams, and I would get a clear bobber, some small hooks, split shot weights, and a jar of salmon eggs for the week. We were ready to go! We caught fish occasionally, but fishing a trout river was a different animal. I couldn't quite figure it out. And then . . .

I was eight years old this particular summer. I remember it like it was yesterday, and it's been over 40 years now. Early one morning I wandered out of our cabin and headed to the river, and standing thigh deep in the bend of The Big Thompson was a real live fly-fisherman. His long bamboo rod was rhythmically swaying back and forth over his head, and some kind of thick line was making loops twenty feet in front of him and then twenty feet behind him. About every fourth cast, he would let the line gently land on the water in front of him, ride the current for a few seconds, and then gently lift it back into the air and begin the rhythmic sway again. It was mesmerizing. I had never seen anything like it. He looked like an artist transported from a time when things were captured in shades of gray. Over his flannel shirt, he had on a well-worn fishing vest with lots of pockets and gadgets. He wore a wide brim hat. He had a small wicker basket attached to a leather strap, which was draped over his left shoulder and hanging at his side. There was a small net just a little bigger than a ping-pong paddle hanging from the back of his vest. And he was wearing hip waders attached to his belt.

I don't know if he saw me or not. I was in a trance. And it appeared he was oblivious to anything other than the river. I just sat there and watched. Caught up in the moment. Feeling like I was in the presence of something great.

The first time he broke rhythm was with a quick jerk of his wrist. In a split second, his rod was bending over. He had hooked a fish. I watched as he patiently pulled the line through the eyelets of his rod about two feet at a time until the fish was within arm's length. He reached behind him with his free hand, grabbed the net, and scooped a beautiful brown trout out of the river. After removing the hook, he slipped the unsuspecting fish into the wicker basket. As if he knew I was there all along, he gave me a thumbs up and a wink. He took a few calculated steps upstream and then went right back into rhythm. I have no idea how long I watched him that morning, but it was long enough to light a fire in my soul that has never been quenched.

That same year, while looking for flat skipping rocks along the bank of the river, I found a piece of floating fly line measuring about eight feet long. I couldn't believe it! I would not have been more excited had it been a gold nugget washed free from a mine up in the mountains. I ran to the cabin, where Grandpa helped me tie the float line onto the end of my Zebco 303 rod and reel. We tied about five feet of four-pound test line to the end of the fly line, and then I begged him to take me to Scott's. With his help, we picked out a few dry flies and headed back to the cabin. I was so excited to be a fly fisherman; I could hardly get to the river fast enough.

With my parent's permission and Grandpa standing close by, I was allowed to be in the river no more than knee deep. It was ice cold in shorts and tennis shoes, but I never gave it a second thought. I was about to fly fish. Now, admittedly, my casts looked nothing like the man I had seen a couple of days before, but within an hour I had figured out how to whip my short graphite rod back and forth with enough strength and timing to get the fly to land on the water ten to twelve feet in front of me. Watching the fly dance on the water and knowing there was a good chance a trout was down below eyeing it made me so happy. I was focused and determined I was going to catch a trout on my new "fly rod"!

Would you believe I caught two trout that year on my homemade, rigged, fly rod contraption? Probably the most rewarding two fish of my life if I had to rank them.

I'm going to move on to the illustration for this chapter, but for my fly-fishing enthusiast friends, you'll be happy to hear that unbeknownst to me, my grandpa had fly-fished earlier in his life, and he presented me with his beautiful two-piece bamboo fly rod the following summer. I have been catching my limit with it for over 40 years now. How about that?!

I share all of this with you because it sets up a life-changing revelation I got when I was in the river a few years ago. Some of you may know that a fly-fisherman doesn't just use any old fly. A wise and experienced angler will assess his surroundings before he selects a fly. What insects are in natural abundance around the river he is fishing? Ants? Grasshoppers? Mayflies? How big are they? What color are they? Do they float or do they sink? And, once he makes these determinations, he selects a fly that mimics what he knows the fish are already seeing and eating.

And why do they eat these flies and insects? Not only were trout designed to eat them, but their very life depends on it. The very things they desire are the things that give them life. How beautifully God created these natural processes. A desire exists, and there is something to satisfy that desire.

Now, here I come with fly rod in hand, entering the river quietly so as not to stir any suspicion. I enter behind a bush, just below the pockets I want to fish. I know the trout are facing upstream and will not see me . . . can you hear the minor chords in the soundtrack as "the enemy" enters the water. I take my time. There's no hurry here. I know the end result if I can get the trout to take my bait.

I put myself in the optimal position to make my first set of casts, knowing the unsuspecting trout is just going to do what comes natural to him. Little does he know what looks like the mayfly he has been eating is actually a counterfeit. It looks like "life" but it has a barbed hook in it, attached to a string, attached to a rod, attached to an enemy who seeks to control him and in very short order . . . kill him.

You may think that's dramatic. It is, certainly. And here's why . . . there is an enemy who has been assessing your surroundings since the day you came into this world. He literally knows you better than you know yourself. He's been fishing this river for years. He knows what you were created to desire and the things that fulfill and sustain your life. And guess what? He is fashioning lures custom made for you. He is subtly sneaking into your life. You don't see him. You're just doing what you do, going about your life. Unsuspecting. He's very observant. He knows when you are most hungry for whatever it is you are craving. What are you craving right now? Affection? Respect? Money? Affirmation? Rest assured there is a counterfeit offer coming to meet that desire. It's going to look like the real thing, and it's going to feel like "life".

Look at these two passages and see how they relate:

> *"Do not gaze at wine when it is red,*
> *when it sparkles in the cup, when it goes down smoothly!*
> *In the end it bites like a snake and poisons like a viper."*
> *Proverbs 23:31-32 (NIV)*

> *"For the lips of the adulterous woman drip honey,*
> *and her speech is smoother than oil;*
> *but in the end she is bitter as gall, sharp as a double-edged sword.*
> *Her feet go down to death; her steps lead straight to the grave."*
> *Proverbs 5:3-5 (NIV)*

Do you see how tempting these things are? It is even written poetically. But check this out from I Peter 5:8 (NIV), " . . . your enemy the devil prowls around like a roaring lion looking for someone to devour." And this, from John 10:10 (NIV), "The thief comes only to steal, kill and destroy . . . ". Those are strong words, men. Prowling. Roaring. Devouring. Stealing. Killing. Destroying.

Here's the deal, guys – God gave us Himself, and He gave us a wife. Our needs are to be met in Him and in her. And, even when you may doubt it, God can and will make up for anything you are not getting from your wife if you will lean into Him. But when those needs and natural desires arise, and they will, beware of the counterfeit bait which leads to death. It may look like the real thing. It may smell like the real thing. It may feel like the real thing. But rest assured, if it does not line up with the entirety of God's Word, it will destroy you. There's a saying that's been around a long time but bears repeating here: "Sin will take you further than you wanted to go, keep you longer than you wanted to stay, and cost you more than you wanted to pay." Beware of the lure!

Since my son was young, when we've seen a beautiful woman on a magazine cover, on a television screen, or on a billboard, I have been quick to say, "Yeah, she's beautiful. But, trust me, she's got issues." You realize, of course, that's safe to say about any woman, or man, on the planet. We all have issues! One big one for certain: we are all sinful. Sometimes, though, we look at the packaging and think, "How could anything be wrong with that?" Aha! You took the bait!

> **SIN WILL TAKE YOU FURTHER THAN YOU WANTED TO GO, KEEP YOU LONGER THAN YOU WANTED TO STAY, AND COST YOU MORE THAN YOU WANTED TO PAY.**

Trust God and make the most of life with the woman He has given you. Any other woman who comes your way has a hook embedded in her, and taking the bait will destroy your life.

✔ Action Point

Take an inventory of the counterfeits in your life when it comes to other women. Who might the enemy use to entice you? Co-workers? Former classmates? Social media contacts on Facebook or Instagram? Pornography?

Don't take the bait! Eliminate the lures so you won't get hooked. Set some serious boundaries around any interaction with women who are not your wife.

▶ Romance Tip

 **"Beautiful Boundaries"**
https://www.youtube.com/watch?v=r7yJScJ3dMQ

Chapter 11

MY DREAM JOB IS A WEDDING PLANNER

Curt

This is Curt, again. Just when you thought it couldn't get any better, you get back to back chapters without Lance. By the way, Lance titled this chapter, not me. I did plan a wedding, and quite honestly, I enjoyed it immensely. You'll see why in the next few pages.

On May 31, 1997, I was at my favorite watering hole, a place called Denim and Diamonds. "D&D" was a country dance bar about three miles from my house. I was a regular there during my first several years in Nashville. I had about four dance partners and I was thinning out the leather soles of my Justin Ropers several nights a week. I was writing country music at the time and playing with a band, so this was a great place for me to unwind in an environment that stoked the creative fires. I was there, literally, at least twice a week, so I was pretty friendly with the other regulars and knew who was who.

On this particular night, as I was doing the "Sweetheart Shadish" with one of my partners, I looked to the side of the dance floor and saw a girl who I had not seen before. Let me put that more accurately – I saw a girl UNLIKE ANY GIRL I had EVER seen before. Do you know that moment? I hope you do. Your stomach drops, you do a double take, your breath catches, and your heart starts racing. All of this happened in an instant, and I was just praying she would still be standing there when the song ended and I left the dance floor. Hallelujah! She was!

I introduced myself and confirmed my suspicion she had never been there before. I asked her if she would like to dance and she confessed she didn't know how to two-step. I said, "No problem, can I teach you?" She smiled and nodded and the rest, as they say, is history!

Now, there's a lot to this story, and in my personal and biased opinion, our story is silver screen worthy. But, for purposes of this book, I'm going to hit a few highlights to set the scene, and then we'll get into how the actual wedding unfolded.

The night I met Emily, she told me she had a six-year old son at home. She told me in a later conversation she was married in her early twenties, fully admitting she just was not equipped at that point in her life to make a marriage work.

Plot Twist

Our friendship grew quickly. We spent a ton of time together. We dated for a year, and during that year I was falling more and more in love but struggling consistently with whether, or not, I could marry a divorced woman and do the whole blended family thing. I know, some of you are ready to close the book right now because you perceive pride and arrogance in that statement. I'll admit there was some. I'm just being honest. By this time, I had grown to love her, her son, John, and I had met her ex-husband on numerous occasions and he seemed like a nice enough guy. But, bottom line, I simply did not have peace about ever getting to the altar. It wasn't fair to her, or to me, to stay in a relationship where I wasn't confident I could close the deal. No doubt one of the hardest things I've ever done was to walk away from this woman who I loved in order to find the peace I knew God intended for me.

Within a few weeks of our break up, God ushered a young lady into my life who "checked all of the boxes" and then some. She was a Baylor University graduate (my alma mater), she was voted a Baylor Beauty (an annual campus calendar showcasing some of the most beautiful female students), she came from a great family in Houston, we had a ton of friends in common, her best friend was married to my college roommate, who is still one of my closest friends, and she probably hadn't missed a quiet time with the Lord since she was in first grade (that may be an exaggeration). Too good to be true, right!?

Wrong. She really was all of that, and I'm sure she has been one heck of a catch for the guy who landed her. But this is the crazy part. The more time I spent with her, the more I fell in love with Emily. I was trying to get my heart to engage with this girl, but it was futile. God, in His wisdom, brought me the girl I thought I had been waiting for my entire life in order to show me that His plan for me was far better. He knew what I *really* wanted, and He definitely knew what I needed! After about five months of trying to fall in love, we both realized it just was not going to happen. We parted amicably, and I felt a peace wash over me there are no words to describe.

Set Free

God had set my heart free to love Emily! I knew I had received His blessing to marry her. And, even beyond His blessing, I was fully convinced it was His will for me to marry her.

I called Emily at her home one evening and asked if I could come over and talk with her about something. She told me later she knew it when she heard my voice on the phone . . . something had changed. Man, had it ever! I felt free to love someone with my whole heart for the first time in my life, and it was exhilarating! Set free to love . . . there's nothing else on earth like it.

Thankfully, Emily still loved me and was very understanding about the detour I had taken in order to be convinced I could move forward with her in complete and total confidence and peace. She could tell I was in a place I had never been before, and she knew I was not one to play games. This gave her the peace and confidence she had needed from me, as well. What an incredible blessing! We were in lock step immediately, and though I had no intention of rushing anything, there was no doubt in my mind I was going to spend the rest of my life with Emily.

SET FREE TO LOVE...THERE'S NOTHING ELSE ON EARTH LIKE IT.

We weren't making wedding plans at all, but we both knew we were headed in that direction. So, it was natural to discuss the future and what it might look like. In regard to a wedding, Emily made it clear the only thing that really mattered to her was that God was the center of it. She didn't need or want any big ceremony – just her, me, the Lord, and her son, John. I off-handedly asked what she would think about me planning it when the time came, and she said that would be great. Man, did my wheels start turning!

One thing I knew for sure – I wanted Emily to feel more loved and more special than she had ever felt in her life. I always thought of her as royalty ... but like the other 99.99+% of the earth's population, she just happened to be born into the wrong family to be Princess Emily and get the royal treatment. So, even though I wasn't royalty either, there was no reason I couldn't treat *her* like it. The plan started to come together in my head, and this is how it unfolded ...

Setting the Stage

In the fall of 1999, about one year after we had started dating again, I gave Emily a gallon sized, clear glass container which had a pillar candle in the middle of it. The rest of the jar was filled with Hershey kisses. There was some decorative ribbon around the glass to give it the "gift" appearance, and there was an envelope inside the jar on top of the candle and kisses. I snuck it into her home one evening when I was over there and hid it until I was ready for the presentation. After dinner, we had settled onto the couch, and I told her there was something I wanted to give her. She's never mentioned that a proposal crossed her mind at that moment. I grabbed the jar from behind the couch, and her eyes lit up.

> SO, EVEN THOUGH I WASN'T ROYALTY EITHER, THERE WAS NO REASON I COULDN'T TREAT HER LIKE IT.

She set the jar on the coffee table and immediately asked what it was for ... I said, "I want you to read the card and then we'll talk about it." In addition to confessing my deepening love for her and my desire to begin taking things to the next level, I told her the idea behind the jar was for her to have "one kiss" a day to remind her of my love for her. And, more importantly, before the kisses were gone, we would be married! Her eyes filled with tears. We hugged. We kissed. And I told her I was the happiest man in the world!

Now, let's be clear . . . I already knew the date of our wedding, and even though it was only about 6 months away, I put over a year's worth of kisses in the jar. Just as I suspected, Emily told me later the first thing she did after I left that night was dump all of the kisses out and count them. According to the kiss count, she knew we would be married sometime before the end of the year 2000.

I've had a romantic fetish with New York City for years. Do you realize how many GREAT romances have happened there? How about these for starters . . . *Breakfast at Tiffany's, An Affair to Remember, West Side Story, You've Got Mail, Sleepless in Seattle, Ghost, When Harry Met Sally, Maid in Manhattan, Hitch, Sweet Home Alabama, Autumn in New York, P.S. I Love You, Enchanted,* and the list goes on and on. The magic just happens in New York!

What I knew was, if I really wanted Emily to be treated like royalty, and if I was willing to pay for it, "It's up to you, New York, New York!" Frank Sinatra, by the way, is my favorite singer of all time. I had an opportunity to make a business trip to Manhattan that same fall,

I WAS GOING AHEAD OF HER AND PREPARING A PLACE AND AN EVENT SHE WOULD NEVER FORGET.

and after booking it I started listing out all of the places I wanted to visit that might be a part of our wedding weekend (hotels, restaurants, entertainment, shopping, etc.). I had every intention of blowing it out of the water.

My trip proved to be more successful than I could have imagined. I was able to visit and book the church where we would be married, as well as the hotel where Emily and I would stay on our wedding night. Keep in mind, Emily only knew I was on a business trip. There was nothing about a wedding in New York that was anywhere on her radar. I was going ahead of her and preparing a place and an event she would never forget.

Start Spreading the News

Now that I had the dates confirmed, when I returned to Nashville, I went to work preparing a guest list and putting the plan together for a surprise wedding. As you might imagine, since Emily was taking a kiss out of her jar every day, the impending wedding was constantly on her mind. There were lots of questions . . . When? Where? What about a dress? What about my hair? And on, and on, and on . . . .

I had one response the entire time, "Emily, trust me, it will be perfect." This did not completely satisfy her, but it's all she got from me. And, even though everything was completely unknown to her, I think deep in her heart she trusted me.

The next tangible clue she received regarding a wedding was on Christmas Day of 1999. I gave her two new pieces of information. The first was a coupon redeemable for 100 kisses that could immediately be pulled out of the jar. This meant she was guaranteed to be married sometime before the end of September of the following year. The second was instructions to have a bag packed and ready to go for a week-long honeymoon in a warm destination. She needed to be ready to go at any moment – there would not be any time to pack once she got the call.

You can imagine the barrage of questions which followed, but staying in character and true to my plan, I responded again, "Emily, trust me, it will be perfect."

In the first week of January 2000, I wrote and mailed 60 very discreet letters to Emily's closest friends and our families with two invitations and a long list of instructions. The first invitation was to write Emily a letter on the stationary I had enclosed . . . to tell her what she meant to them, how she had impacted their life, and how thrilled they were to hear she was getting married, and that they would be praying for her on April 15th. After writing the letter to Emily, they were to seal it and return it to me in the enclosed stamped and addressed envelope. Everyone knew these letters were to be a surprise for Emily on the day before her wedding.

The second invitation was to actually join us for our wedding in New York on April 15, 2000. I was very clear that Emily would not know anything about it until April 14th and that they were sworn to secrecy. I let them know they were invited because of how much they meant to Emily and/or to me. If they wanted to plan a fun weekend in New York in the middle of April and make attending our wedding part of their trip, we would be honored to have them. I was shocked and humbled to discover within a few weeks of sending the letters out, I had confirmations from 42 people who planned to be in New York to celebrate with us . . . unbelievable!!!

The Game Plan

Now it was time to start planning the perfect weekend for Emily. Even as I write this my heart is racing. It may have been the most fun I have had in my entire life. I was not going to spare any expense. The sky was the limit. Once I determined the things that would bless Emily the most, it was just a matter of working it into her schedule while she was in New York. Let the fun begin . . .

One thing I knew for sure was Emily needed to share the events of this weekend with someone. The obvious choice for me was her best friend, Jill, whom I had also grown to love over the past three years. While Emily is reserved, a little passive, and a total rule follower, Jill is incredibly adventurous, resourceful, and will make someone tell her "no" three or four times before she really believes they mean it. And, just to be fair, there aren't many people who tell Jill "no". She's just a person to whom you want to say "yes." She was the perfect person to help pull off everything I wanted to happen for Emily in The Big Apple. And I knew she could talk Emily into pretty much anything. I had heard plenty of stories about their adventures together, and if it came down to needing to keep Emily on a schedule or get her somewhere she might not initially feel like going, Jill could get it done. When I shared the plan with Jill, she was ecstatic and said she would be more than happy to help!

I called our pastor, Scott Patty, and shared the plan with him. I told him we would be so honored if he would perform the ceremony, but that I completely understood if it was too big of an ask. I was so blessed when he said he would make it happen. This was a significant piece for a couple of reasons . . . Scott was the guy who prayed with Emily when she made a decision to surrender her life to Jesus. Scott was the guy who performed her baptism after she shared her testimony with friends and family. And Scott was the first pastor to really teach the Bible to Emily in a way that made it come alive for her. So, needless to say, his presence and participation in our wedding would be HUGE for Emily. He and I worked out the details and I got his flight and hotel booked for that weekend. Hallelujah!

The next thing I wanted to get done was Emily's itinerary while she was in Manhattan. It was going to be important that everyone attending the wedding would know where she was at all times so they could avoid running into her. I know that sounds crazy . . . after all, it's New York. But I didn't want to take any chances at ruining this great surprise for my bride. So, I had Emily's hour by hour plan in place, printed out, and mailed to all of the people coming to the wedding. Knowing where she was going to be ahead of time would allow them the freedom to plan a great weekend in the city without fear of bumping into Emily.

I recommended a couple of hotels for our guests that were in the city, but not too close to The Plaza Hotel, where Emily and Jill would be staying – a famous hotel on Fifth Avenue overlooking Central Park. And I gave them a few recommendations of touristy things they might enjoy based on my research of the city. As luck would have it, the Yankees were playing the Kansas City Royals at Yankee Stadium on the Friday night before our wedding, so I got tickets for about 20 of us. We would take the subway to the ball game, watch Derek Jeter, David Justice, Bernie Williams and the rest of the Yanks in their pinstripes. And during the 7th inning stretch, I had it set up for the scoreboard in centerfield to light up with, "Congratulations Curt & Emily!" I knew I could get a picture to put in our scrapbook and show Emily later since she would have no idea any of this was going on.

So, let's get to it . . . I told Emily a couple of weeks in advance of our surprise wedding date that I had booked an out of town golf trip with two of my buddies, Kevin Wagley and Paul Dott. This was not unusual. We planned to leave on Thursday, April 13, after work, and would play Friday and Saturday before heading back to Nashville. I think this was one of only a handful of lies I actually had to tell in order to pull this off. Well, you guessed it, I'm sure – Kevin, Paul and I boarded a plane to New York on the evening of the 13th. As far as Emily knew, I was in East Tennessee on a golf trip. I called her that night to tell her goodnight and that I loved her – knowing in a few hours she would be awakened by the phone again, with a call she had been waiting on for a long time!

Wake Up Call

At 3:30am, on Friday, April 14, 2000, I called Emily and woke her out of a dead sleep. After she mumbled, "Hello?" I said, "Baby, it's time." She came out of her stupor quickly and said, "What do you mean?" I

Top: Curt holding Emily's ring on the Thursday afternoon plane ride from Nashville to New York City with friends Paul Dott (L) and Kevin Wagley (R).
Bottom: The scoreboard at Yankee Stadium boasting "Congratulations Curt & Emily" at Friday night's game vs. the Kansas City Royals.

said, "It's time. Your ride is going to be there in two and a half hours to pick you up. Dress comfortably, but fashionably (never a stretch for Emily), and be ready to go by 6:00 when your ride shows up. I have everything set for John, just make sure he's up and dressed. And bring the suitcase you have packed for our honeymoon." I remember her words as her mind was already racing with the unknowns. She said, "Why do you do this to me?" I laughed, told her I loved her, and that I would see her in a few hours. We hung up, and I thought to myself, here we go . . . and I'm the luckiest man in the world!

At 3:40am, Emily called her best friend Jill to share the news about the phone call she had just received. Jill acted surprised and asked questions that Emily didn't know the answers to – and Emily had no idea *Jill knew* all of the answers. Unbeknownst to Emily, Jill was already awake, bags packed and headed to the airport. She and her husband were on the flight to New York that would arrive one hour ahead of Emily's.

At 6:00am, there was a knock on the door of Emily's condo. She opened it to find the smiling faces of her folks, Nancy and Glenn. They all exchanged hugs and tried to encourage nine-year-old John, who didn't quite understand the confusion of a very atypical morning. Bags were loaded into the car and the four of them were off to the next destination, still unknown to Emily. Per my instructions, Glenn and Nancy were faithful to answer all of Emily's questions with, "Curt said not to worry, and to tell you everything will be perfect." I'm sure this was met with repeated eyerolls, but she had been hearing the same thing for several months, so she was used to it.

Within 30 minutes they pulled into the Nashville International Airport. Emily now knew she was getting on a flight. When they got inside the airport, Nancy gave Emily her plane ticket with the destination of LaGuardia Airport in New York, New York? What?!? She had never been to New York before . . . how exciting! Headline reads . . . "Small Town Girl Goes to the Big City!"

This was pre-9/11, so all four of them walked to the departure gate. To distract John, Nancy took him aside and assured him that he had a major surprise coming. He could not let his mom know, but in just a few hours, he would be getting on a plane to New York, too!

With excited hugs, they said their farewells and told Emily to have a great time – they would be praying for her. Nancy gave Emily a gift bag and told her to open it once she was seated on the plane. When Emily settled into her seat, she opened the gift bag and found a stack of identical envelopes, rubber banded together, and each envelope was marked with a time to be opened. On her two-hour flight from Nashville to New York, Emily read one letter about every 10 minutes from one of her closest friends or family members who expressed their love for her and shared their excitement regarding her trip to New York for a wedding. Some of them coyly shared how they wished they could be there, or that they would look forward to seeing her and hearing about everything when she got back. She still had no clue there was going to be a big-time celebration in New York! Most of the people she was reading letters from were also enroute to the wedding weekend. But they knew Emily's flight schedule, so they were all careful to book flights that would not have them in the airports at the same time she was there. Too good . . .

Welcome to the Big Apple

With growing excitement, as she neared landing in New York, the last envelope Emily opened was from me. In addition to telling her I hoped she had enjoyed the flight, reading all of the letters from people who loved her, I also gave her instructions to head to baggage claim when she landed at LaGuardia. There would be someone waiting for her there with instructions.

One of the first things Emily noticed at baggage claim was that there was an Asian man with a video camera, who appeared to be capturing some footage of her. She didn't know why, but ignored it. As she turned toward the luggage carousel, she couldn't believe her eyes . . . JILL!!! They both screamed, and Emily said, "What are you doing here?" Jill laughed and said, "I'll be spending the weekend with you – let's get your bag, our limo is right outside." The videographer, Leo, was hired by me to capture everything I was going to be missing during the weekend. So, the three of them loaded into the limo. Jill gave Emily a dozen red roses from me and said, "Curt told me to tell you he loves you, he can't wait to see you, and that everything is going to be perfect!"

The first stop for the limo was the County Clerk's office in Manhattan. Our marriage license had to be signed within 48 hours of the wedding ceremony. I met Emily out front with a major hug and kiss – I was so relieved to actually know she was safely in New York, with Jill, and that all of my plans were about to unfold for her. Within about 30 minutes we had the marriage license signed and notarized, and I sent her on her way with a kiss and the assurance I would be going ahead of her all weekend to make sure everything was perfect. And, most importantly, that I would see her the following night for our wedding!

> "CURT TOLD ME TO TELL YOU HE LOVES YOU, HE CAN'T WAIT TO SEE YOU, AND THAT EVERYTHING IS GOING TO BE PERFECT!"

The limo took the girls to The Plaza Hotel. This place is POSH! I had already been in their room, which overlooked Central Park, and had a vase of roses on the dresser with an attached note. On the bed, there was another envelope with Emily's name on it. Inside were directions to three department stores within walking distance. Each of these stores sold wedding dresses, and I felt confident the 15 crisp $100 bills enclosed in the card would allow her to get a dress and shoes she would look and feel great in.

Let me summarize the next few hours quickly, but with enough details to help you understand the point Lance is going to make in the next chapter.

Friday

- Dress shopping on Fifth Avenue (successful, by the way, including tailoring)
- Relax at the Plaza Hotel
- Get ready for a night on the town
- Picked up by horse and carriage outside of the hotel for a ride through Central Park
- Dropped off by carriage for dinner reservations at the renowned Tavern on the Green restaurant in Central Park
- I left the late-night agenda open, but gave Jill some suggestions for things I thought Emily might enjoy. They went to a restaurant on top of one of the skyscrapers to have dessert and savor a stellar view of the city.

On Saturday morning, I was up really early and super pumped for the events of the day. I walked from my hotel, The Park Central, to the Plaza Hotel. On the way, I bought a bouquet of fresh flowers from a corner shop. When I got to the hotel, I placed an order with room service for an incredible breakfast and had it delivered to Emily and Jill's room with the flowers and a big-time love note from me.

Top: Jill (L) and Emily (R) on their horse drawn carriage ride through Central Park on their way to dinner at Tavern on the Green Friday evening.
Bottom: Emily getting her wedding day pedicure at the Oscar Blondie Salon inside the infamous Plaza Hotel.

Per my specific instructions to Jill, she and Emily left the room mid-morning for shoe shopping, walking the streets of Manhattan, and lunch. While they were out and about, I went back to the Plaza Hotel to make a slight change in Emily's accommodations. With the help of a maître d', I removed all of Emily's personal belongings from the room she was in, and had them transferred to our honeymoon suite. This suite had it all . . . the view of Fifth Avenue, a sitting room that could accommodate 15-20 people easily, a gas fireplace that was always burning, a beautiful chandelier, ornate trim, and marble everything! When Emily returned from shopping, ready to prepare herself for the wedding, she was going to do it in complete and total luxury!

Jill knew the appointments I had lined up at the Oscar Blondie Salon, located inside the Plaza – so, she had Emily back in plenty of time to make her manicure, pedicure, and her appointment with a top hair stylist who could do absolutely anything Emily wanted done for the wedding. This was pampering at its finest. Everything was paid for, everyone involved knew the story, and they took great pleasure in making Emily feel like a princess!

After leaving the spa, Emily went back to the honeymoon suite to get dressed. I had informed her I would be at the hotel to pick her up by 5:00pm. I called her from the lobby at 5:00 sharp, and when she told me she was ready, I told her I would come to the room because I had a question I needed to ask her.

I'll never forget the smile on her face or the way time seemed to stop when I saw her standing there in that dress, glowing like an angel, perfectly made up from head to toe. It was everything either of us could have dreamed it would be. I walked her inside the room and dropped to one knee. With tears in my eyes, I confessed my love for her and my intention to make her feel like a princess for as long as I lived, and I asked her if she would take my hand in marriage. SHE SAID, "YES!!!"

We're Getting Married

After a quick swing through the Oscar Blondie Salon so all of the spa attendants could see the finished product and meet the groom, we walked through the lobby of the hotel and out to our limo. It felt like a fairytale ... truly a magical moment. We were only a few blocks from the Central Presbyterian Church in Manhattan, where we would be wed. It was a church commissioned and funded by John D. Rockefeller in 1922, and has since been used for a number of feature films. It is the quintessential cathedral style church.

As we were pulling up to the church, the door swung open to a smiling Pastor Scott Patty ... Emily gasped as she stepped out of the limo, and said, "What are you doing here?" Scott said he heard we were getting married and needed a pastor to perform the ceremony. We all hugged and then walked inside. In the lobby of the church, Jill and her husband, Bill, were waiting on us. Emily screamed again when she saw Bill ... "How long have you been here?" She had no idea Bill had been in New York the past two days.

The five of us prayed together in the lobby of the church, and then I told Emily that when I opened the doors to the sanctuary, I wanted her to step inside and just pause for a moment ... to take in a sight she would never forget.

As the huge arched wooden doors opened, the pianist began to play, and standing in front of Emily were 42 candlelit faces of her family and closest friends who had all come to New York to be a part of her wedding. Every face was visible. They were standing in a "V" formation, each one holding a candle, and at the apex of the V, at the front of the church, was her son, John, waiting on her to walk the aisle so he could hug her neck. Emily gasped, her knees buckled, and we all cried tears of joy!

Top Left: Emily getting ready for the wedding in our suite at the Plaza Hotel.
Top Right: Emily receiving Curt's call from the lobby of the Plaza Hotel stating he needed to come up to her room and ask her a BIG question.
Bottom: Friends and family from across the country who came to celebrate with us and surprise Emily for the wedding ceremony.

Clockwise From Top Left

1. Emily's first glance at all of these surprise guests buckled her knees and sobs insued.

2. Emily looking at each guest in disbelief.

3. Praying to begin the ceremony with Pastor Scott Patty.

4. Curt presenting Emily's son, John, with a cross necklace as a covenant symbol of marriage.

Top: Pastor Scott making the marriage official before God, family and friends.
Bottom: The official first kiss of Curt and Emily Campbell's marriage.

The service was simple, beautiful, worshipful, informal and yet as ceremonious and holy as any I have ever witnessed. There were no attendants, there was no rehearsal, just the people we loved worshipping together as we shared our hearts with each other. Our pre-marital counselors and dear friends, David and Elaine Atchison, both gave us a charge regarding marriage. One of our dearest friends, Chris Bryson, led us in worship, accompanied on piano by another great friend, Chris Davis. The men prayed over me, and the women prayed over Emily. I gave John a cross necklace during the ceremony and shared with him the significance of the covenant I was making with his mom and with him. Emily and I shared the vows we had written, and Pastor Scott made it all official in the eyes of God and the State of New York.

My videographer, Leo, captured it all beautifully, and several people were taking pictures. We have relished the memories of those moments ever since!

Post-ceremony we all walked about three blocks to the Seventh Regiment Armory, a National Historic Landmark, where we had a wonderful dinner together, and where everyone finally had the opportunity to talk with Emily openly about the months of secrets that had been kept from her. We thanked all of our friends and family, cut the cake, prayed together, and then dismissed folks to go enjoy New York or to feel free to join us in our suite for a couple of hours to share highlights from the weekend. Most of our family came to hang out with us at The Plaza for a little while, and when we finally closed the door on the last guest, Emily and I fell into each other's arms in complete joy and emotional exhaustion.

Our seven-night honeymoon at an all-inclusive resort in Cancun, Mexico, was icing on the cake . . . but the entire wedding week was, and still is, a frequent topic of conversation.

Now why, in a book written for men, would I go into such great detail about a wedding? And not just the wedding itself, but all of the minute details and planning leading up to the wedding? And, just for the record, I left out a lot!

This story, believe it or not, relates to you in a very personal way. Lance is going to share that in the next chapter ... I hope it blesses you!

✅ Action Point

Relive your own wedding story with your wife this week. I'm sure she'll be shocked that you initiate this idea. If you have a photo album, a video, or any other memorabilia from your wedding, get it out and enjoy it together. Tell her you would do it all over again, and that you are still amazed she chose you.

▶ Romance Tip

 **"Framed"**

https://www.youtube.com/watch?v=H1eXL11Geg4

Chapter 12

A BETTER WEDDING THAN CURT'S

Lance

Men, let me start by simply saying "I'm sorry". Sorry that Curt is so extra. Sorry he is so over the top. You need to understand the only way he was ever going to get Emily to agree to marry him was to put her in such an unreal situation that she would really have no choice but to go through with the wedding. The rest of us normal guys did not use all these "smoke and mirror" tactics to convince our wives to marry us. The most amazing part of Curt's whole story is the fact Emily has chosen to stay married to him all these years!

Okay, seriously, we do have to tip our hat to Curt's wedding extravaganza. And I am guessing there are a few of you men who would like to hire him for your upcoming wedding and surprise your fiancé. I am sure, for the right price, Curt would be happy to vicariously live out his wedding planner dreams through you! However, before we jump on a plane and head to The Plaza honeymoon suite in New York, let's take a look back at Curt and Emily's amazing wedding story and see if there might be a few correlations to an even more amazing wedding between Christ and us.

We Think There Is A Better Option

Early in Curt and Emily's dating relationship they broke up because Curt had commitment issues (actually Curt has a lot of issues . . . not just commitment) and had some doubts. While they were apart Curt dated what seemed to be the perfect girl for him. On paper she was the type of girl he was looking for and who could, and should, make him happy. But something wasn't quite right. He kept thinking about Emily.

Have you ever done this with the Lord? I have. Even though I really like God and enjoy my time with him, I am just not sure I want to make a lifetime commitment. Besides, there are a lot of other things out there that sure do look like they would make me just as happy as God. What about having money? With all my debt it sure seems like winning the lottery would cure all my issues. Back in college, struggling to find a date, I really thought if I could find a girl my life would be perfect and complete. Or what about work? Once I get that promotion, then I will have more control of my schedule and time for family. That is when it will all come together for me. The problem for us men is we keep looking everywhere but to God for what only God can give us.

The reality is the grass may look greener on the other side, but it still has to be mowed. I have totally treated my relationship with Christ like Curt did with Emily when they first started dating. I was scared to death if I really committed my life to Christ, then He would call me to be a missionary to some remote part of Africa. I will be honest with you . . . I don't have the legs to wear those loincloth tribal shorts, and I like Chick-fil-a too much to live outside the United States. My doubts kept me from trusting that Christ was the One for me! Sound familiar, Curt?

Curt was running from commitment due to fears of the unknown, but what he found he could not run from was his love for Emily. Similarly, my fears of what God would require of me caused me to run from Him, but what I could not overcome was my growing love for Him and His completed act of love for me on the cross. I am so thankful for God's patience with my fears, and my stupidity, during those early years of discovering my faith and deepening in my understanding of myself and Christ.

> **AS WE FULLY UNDERSTAND AND EVEN EXPERIENCE HIS LOVE FOR US, IT IGNITES IN OUR HEARTS A LOVE FOR HIM.**

You see, Curt finally realized his love for Emily far outweighed any potential unknowns and fears of living a lifetime without her. This is how it is in our walk with Christ. As we fully understand and even experience His love for us, it ignites in our hearts a love for Him. We no longer live out our faith from a position of obligation, but from a position of adoration and love. We don't think of our relationship with Christ as something I have to do, but something I get to do . . . something I want to do!

Why Is It So Hard to Trust Him?

I will never know how Emily trusted Curt so completely with such a big day. All she ever got was "Emily, trust me, it is going to be perfect". To my knowledge this was Curt's one and only attempt at wedding planning, and yet Emily gave him the keys to the whole deal. She must have been crazy. But what if Emily wasn't crazy at all? What if she had grown to love and trust Curt to the point of knowing he will do everything to make it the best? Maybe she realized Curt had her best interest at heart, and that allowed her to let go and just enjoy the journey and the experience.

It is so good when I can do this same thing with God. When I am able to trust Him because I know His love for me and fully believe He has what is best for me in mind. Emily would have probably never put together the kind of wedding Curt did. She would have never dreamed of something so lavish and over the top. Similarly, there have been times in my life when God has done things far beyond anything I would have imagined for myself and our family. All I had to do was trust Him.

Again, my life verse is Proverbs 3:5-6, and it speaks to this very act of trusting the Lord:

> *"Trust in Lord with all your heart,*
> *and do not lean on your own understanding.*
> *In all your ways acknowledge Him,*
> *And He will make your paths straight."*
> *Proverbs 3:5-6 (NASB)*

We are to trust Him with all our hearts because trusting with our brains, or physical abilities, will only leave us falling short. It will also leave us thinking we had something to do with the outcomes. That we were somehow smart enough or strong enough to make it all come together. Yet this Proverb tells us to trust with all our hearts. Because God knows if He has our heart, everything else will follow.

Notice, too, that not everything will make sense along way. We may not be able to have a clear understanding of what God is up to, but trusting Him allows us to enjoy even the toughest and wildest journeys in our lives. All along Emily's wedding journey, she had things she did not understand and there were more than a few moments of shock, joy, and I am guessing anxiety, as well. Yet through it all, she continued to trust Curt's lead. And I know she is glad she did. As close friends of Curt and Emily, it is still fun to sometimes ask them to share parts of their wedding story with new friends who have never heard it. Emily always smiles and lights up at the thought of telling all Curt did to make her feel like a "princess".

The beauty of surrendering our hearts and our control fully to Christ is that He is creating the most incredible wedding story for our lives. He is simply and softly saying, "Lance, trust me, it is going to be perfect." The entirety of the Bible is this love story of God's never-ending pursuit of me, and of YOU. We (man & woman) broke up with Him in the garden right at the beginning of all of creation. How? We sinned. But our sin set in motion the greatest journey of redemption ever! The greatest wedding story of all time! We are reminded of this whole journey in John 3:16 (NASB):

> *"For God so loved the world (that is you and me), that He gave His only begotten Son, that whoever believes in Him, shall not perish, but have eternal life."*

I heard Andy Stanley put it this way. God Loved . . . God Gave . . . We Believe . . . We Receive. When I share with coaches and athletes, I put it another way. I call this the ABC's of God's love:

A—Admit

We are not perfect. That we have sinned. Romans 3:23 "For all have sinned and fallen short of the kingdom of God." Notice it does not say "some" or a "few". It says "all" of us have sinned. No one is perfect. No one is deserving of a big wedding in New York!

B—Believe

Christ lived perfectly and died sacrificially. Romans 6:23 (NASB) "For the wages for sin is death, but the gift of God is eternal life in Christ Jesus our Lord." A wage is something you work for. Something you earn. What we earn for our sin is death. This is not just a physical death, but a spiritual death that leaves us separated from God and His love for eternity. A gift is something you don't earn. Something you don't deserve. We have earned death, but God gives us eternal life through the gift of His Son. All we have to do is trust Him.

C—Commit

God has done all the work. He has planned out the whole "wedding". The only thing we have to do is trust Him and, by faith, commit to a covenant, growing relationship with Christ. When Curt and Emily exchanged their vows and placed rings on each other's hands, they were making a commitment to one another. Their commitment was not made from obligation, but from love. Their commitment to love one another was not because they had to ... their commitment to love one another was because they wanted to more than anything else! We have to quit trying to earn God's love by living by rules and regulations. Christianity is NOT about moral behavior, but about heart transformation. Fall in love with Christ at the altar, and then grow in His love each and every day.

CHRISTIANITY IS NOT ABOUT MORAL BEHAVIOR, BUT ABOUT HEART TRANSFORMATION.

No doubt Curt's wedding story is cool and probably one for a Hallmark movie, but God's loving pursuit of us is cooler than any movie. It is the greatest love story of all time! Men, you will never fully love your wife the way we have talked about in this book until you have fully surrendered your life to Christ. You want to know how to really forgive, really love unconditionally, and really be a great husband? It all starts at the foot of the Cross. Jesus loves you the way you need to love her! Now go . . . Love Him, and He will help you truly Love Your Wife!

✅ Action Points

If, after reading this book, you realize the real issue in your marriage is YOUR heart, and you are sick and tired of being sick and tired, then Curt and I challenge you to not only surrender your heart to Christ by faith, but to get up this coming Sunday morning and go to church. You may not have been to church in years, or ever, but find a faith community that teaches from the Bible. See if your wife will go with you, AND take your kids, as well.

Maybe they have been going to church without you for years … get up this Sunday, get dressed and be waiting in the car to drive your family to church. They may look shocked and confused. Your wife may even tear up (probably because she has been praying for this day, but never thought it would happen). Just smile and say, "Can we park in the visitor parking spot since I am going to church today?"

The point is … get plugged into a community of Christ followers who are going to encourage you as a man, husband and dad. You can't do this alone!

▶ Romance Tip

"A Word in the Word"
https://www.youtube.com/watch?v=Pv3-KEkFoRU&t=53s

CLOSING

So, now what? Here are a few action points to continue the journey of loving your wife:

1. Spend some time with God daily. Remember, we will never love our wives fully until we are loving Jesus with all we've got. Start with a daily devotional.
2. If you are not in a local church, find one. Get plugged in and join a small couples group or class for fellowship and encouragement.
3. Join the Love Your Wife movement by receiving our encouragement in your email and on your social media accounts. We will send you occasional ideas to help you creatively communicate your love to your wife.
4. Recruit some guys to join you on this journey. Hold each other accountable to love your wives intentionally and consistently.
5. Stay in touch with us and let us know how you are doing.

ABOUT
LOVE YOUR WIFE

Website: www.loveyourwife.net
Facebook: @loveyourwifeofficial
Instagram: @lywofficial
YouTube: Subscribe using the link
on our website homepage

The team at LOVEYOURWIFE is committed to helping you...not to make your marriage better, but to make your marriage NEW! Our coaches, Curt and Lance, will help you be the very best husband you can be.

Join a community of men who are committed to re-capturing the FIRE we all had on our wedding day - before the routine and pressure of life started dousing the flames of love and romance.

Marriage is hard and requires consistent effort and perseverance to have success. Going it alone is a recipe for disaster. Sometimes all it takes is a word of encouragement, someone cheering you on, or a fresh idea or perspective to effectively LOVE YOUR WIFE. That's what LoveYourWife.net is all about.

ABOUT
LANCE BROWN

Lance got his start in ministry with the Fellowship of Christian Athletes in August of 1991. He served for 10 years on staff with FCA in Nashville, TN as the Assistant Area Director. During his last six years with FCA, Lance began working closely with the athletes and coaches at Vanderbilt University.

In the summer of 2001, Lance founded WhoUWith? Ministries where he currently still serves as Director. Lance began by serving the athletes and coaches on the campus of Vanderbilt University, but WhoUWith? Ministries has now grown to six staff serving the greater Nashville area at Vanderbilt University, Belmont University as well as providing the new team chaplain for the Tennessee Titans. Lance's work has also grown beyond just the Nashville area as he regularly invests in the lives of coaches at Clemson, Penn State, Arizona State, Notre Dame and Texas. He also meets with sports chaplains from across the southeast for encouragement and sharing of his 25+ years of sports ministry experience.

Lance is a popular speaker for churches, athletic teams, corporations and summer camps. He has been the keynote speaker for the Fellowship of Christian Athletes National Camps, including St. Simon's Leadership Camp, Boy's Black Mountain Camp and Captain's Camp for leaders in the Georgia and North Carolina. Lance also is a sought after communicator for men's events and corporate leadership meetings.

Lance graduated from Belmont University School of Business in 1991 and is an ordained minister. Lance, and his wife, Aimee have been married since July '92 and live in Goodlettsville, TN. They have five children Shelby, Bailey and Coby (son-in-law), Kelsey and Cooper. Lance is passionate about loving and romancing his bride, leading his family and serving collegiate athletes and coaches.

Cooper, Kelsey, Shelby, Aimee, Lance, Naomi (granddaughter), Bailey and Coby (Zoe the family dog and mascot)

ABOUT
CURT CAMPBELL

Curt has lived in Nashville, Tennessee, since 1992. He moved here to chase a songwriting dream and ended up falling in love with Music City. He grew up in Denton, Texas, and graduated from Baylor University, but if it's true that "home is where the heart is," the Rocky Mountains of Colorado are definitely his home. He's found his way to the mountains every year since he was born. Knee deep in a trout stream, with a fly rod in his hands, is his little piece of Heaven on earth.

Curt is an ordained minister and has been in prison ministry since 2005, trying to encourage men to become all God designed them to be. A significant piece of that is helping them understand the role of a husband and a father. In addition to working with men inside and coming out of prison, he enjoys pre-marriage and marriage counseling, as well as leading love and romance workshops for men.

Curt married an unbelievable Tennessee girl, the love of his life, in the year 2000. He and Emily are blessed with a son, John and his wife, Sarah; and a daughter, McKay and her husband, John David. One of the greatest passions of Curt's life is learning how to love his wife better and be intentional with his children. He admits he has failed many times, but he is committed to getting better and better.

He and his longtime friend, Lance, have been great encouragers to each other through the years as they have basically competed to see who can be the better husband. The competition is fun, but the encouragement is priceless. They both agree they are better men and better husbands because of their friendship. And, as a result, their wives and children are the direct beneficiaries.

Back row: McKay (daughter) and husband John David Moffitt, John Marlin (son) and wife Sarah. Front row: Curt and Emily Campbell

Made in the USA
Monee, IL
18 June 2022